Advanced Introduction to Globalisation

Elgar Advanced Introductions are stimulating and thoughtful introductions to major fields in the social sciences and law, expertly written by the world's leading scholars. Designed to be accessible yet rigorous, they offer concise and lucid surveys of the substantive and policy issues associated with discrete subject areas.

The aims of the series are two-fold: to pinpoint essential principles of a particular field, and to offer insights that stimulate critical thinking. By distilling the vast and often technical corpus of information on the subject into a concise and meaningful form, the books serve as accessible introductions for undergraduate and graduate students coming to the subject for the first time. Importantly, they also develop well-informed, nuanced critiques of the field that will challenge and extend the understanding of advanced students, scholars and policymakers.

For a full list of titles in the series please see the back of the book. Recent titles in the series include:

Advanced Introduction to

Globalisation

JONATHAN MICHIE

*Professor of Innovation and Knowledge Exchange, Director of the
Department for Continuing Education and President of Kellogg College,
University of Oxford, UK*

Elgar Advanced Introductions

Cheltenham, UK • Northampton, MA, USA

Published by
Edward Elgar Publishing Limited
The Lypiatts
15 Lansdown Road
Cheltenham
Glos GL50 2JA
UK

Edward Elgar Publishing, Inc.
William Pratt House
9 Dewey Court
Northampton
Massachusetts 01060
USA

A catalogue record for this book
is available from the British Library

Library of Congress Control Number: 2016962545

ISBN 978 1 78471 069 9 (cased)
ISBN 978 1 78471 071 2 (paperback)
ISBN 978 1 78471 070 5 (eBook)

Typeset by Servis Filmsetting Ltd, Stockport, Cheshire

Printed on FSC approved paper

Printed and bound in Great Britain by Marston Book Services Ltd, Oxfordshire

Contents

About the author

Jonathan Michie is Professor of Innovation and Knowledge Exchange at the University of Oxford where he is Director of the Department for Continuing Education and President of Kellogg College. He is a Fellow of the Academy of Social Sciences. He is also a Council member of the United World Colleges (UWC) movement, and Chair of Governors for UWC Atlantic College.

Dedication

This book is dedicated to my wife, Carolyn Downs, and to our sons Alex and Duncan.

Preface and acknowledgements

> Why should I care about future generations? What have they ever done
> for me?
> (Groucho Marx)

> When aggregated wealth demands what is unfair, its immense power can
> be met only by the still greater power of the people as a whole.
> (Franklin D. Roosevelt)

Globalisation impacts almost all aspects of our lives. Smartphones give access to news, documents, and communications instantaneously and globally. It is said that change is accelerating, and the nation state is increasingly anachronistic. This book challenges that consensus. Globalisation is as old as capitalism, as is technological change. The reduced power of national governments is due to the free-market form of globalisation created by the 1980s era of Thatcher and Reagan, which caused the 2008–2009 global financial crisis and recession. We need to move beyond this, taxing wealth and speculation to create a new era of sustainable development, globally. I am grateful to the following for various support and assistance in the writing of this book:

The British Academy and the Leverhulme Trust for jointly funding my research project on 'Conceptualising and evaluating the potential and actual benefits of mutualism as a business model', and my co-researchers on that project Daniel Tischer, Ruth Yeoman, Stuart White, and Alex Nicholls (on which, see Tischer et al., 2016). The University of Oxford and Kellogg College's Governing Body for granting me sabbatical leave. The European University Institute, Italy, and the University of the Witwatersrand, Johannesburg, for appointing me to Visiting Professorships, to enable me to work on this book.

Dr Martin Ruhs, Associate Professor of Political Economy at the University of Oxford's Department for Political Economy, for his insights on migration, and for developing a series of online courses on political economy, including on globalisation. Anthony Haden-West, an ex-Wall Street Trader for his thoughts on the way that tax evasion is leading to capital being in effect withdrawn from productive use. My various co-authors on globalisation, most notably Daniele Archibugi, Jeremy Howells, Michael Kitson, and Vishnu Padayachee. Colleagues from UWC Atlantic College, and the United World Colleges movement globally, for inspiration. (All royalties from this book will go to UWC Atlantic College's scholarship fund.)

Colleagues at Edward Elgar Publishing, including Matthew Pitman and Rachel Downie for commissioning and delivering this book; the editors of my two book series with Edward Elgar (on globalisation, and on the modern corporation); and Rachel Martin, the Project Editor for my three-volume collection on globalisation and democracy. Raees Chowdhury for research assistance, and my PA, Sandra Gee for her excellent organisational skills and general assistance.

My wife Carolyn Downs, who demonstrates on a daily basis that people's lives can be improved through intelligent and active public policy, currently as Chief Executive of the London Borough of Brent, the most diverse area in Europe; and who put up with me completing this book on holiday. And our sons, Alex and Duncan, likewise – at the time of writing, Duncan editing his student newspaper and campaigning to prevent a fellow student from being deported; and Alex, having escaped from South Sudan in July 2016 just before the airport was closed, where he and his girlfriend Sophie had been working as ODI Fellows, then served on the UWC Atlantic College lifeboat in the Mediterranean, assisting with refugees in danger at sea, before returning to Africa. With apologies to Alex and Duncan for the state of the world they're inheriting from our generation, but with optimism for the future, given the commitment of them and their friends.

1   Introduction: what's going on and what's it all about?

> We cannot solve problems by using the same kind of thinking we used when we created them.
>
> (Albert Einstein)

As someone once said, the times they are a changin. Last year I went back to Edinburgh for a 40th-reunion of leaving school – not as posh as it sounds – just a bunch of us in a pub reminiscing about how rubbish the school had been. The only downside of such events is that not everyone was still with us – one had died of a drug overdose, and the rest from motorbike accidents. From what I remember of the time, that's probably not unsurprising. Fast-forward forty years and today's newspaper had a small article about a school-mate of our younger son, from the local comprehensive – he hadn't died, but he was reported as having written an online post he wanted to be remembered as his final words, should he be killed; he had moved to Syria, and although he denied it, the media had reported that he'd joined Islamic State, and his parents in Oxford were awaiting trial after being charged with terrorism offences relating to allegedly sending their son money.[1]

So, where does one start? No-one from our class did that. But then, online posts hadn't been invented.

The whole mass of developments that have created today's world, which seems so transformed from earlier eras, with the speed of change if anything accelerating, of which this story is just one small illustration, are often subsumed under the description or explanation of 'globalisation' – the 'end of the nation state', living in a 'global village', the world 'is flat', and so on.[2]

---

1 See the *Guardian*, 26 July 2016.

2 I wrote this sentence with no specific proponents, authors or publications in mind, but as it happens, *The End of the Nation State* is the title of Kenichi Ohmae's 1995 book; 'global village' is a term associated with Marshall McLuhan; and *The World is Flat* is the title of Thomas Friedman's 2005 book.

Over the past few years we seem to have witnessed great globalisation developments with the international migration of people; the advent and development of the Internet and other technologies that permit global communication instantaneously; international finance having free rein to roam the globe as it pleases; the continued growth of trade; the breaking down of barriers to the global market-place – and so on across the economy, technology, society, politics and the arts.

But how much of this is new? So what – does it matter? And what if anything can and should we be doing about it?

These are the questions that the current book seeks to answer. The book reports on the latest research on these issues from academics, but also comments on current developments, and considers the big questions of what has gone wrong with the world and what might be done to fix it. The focus of the book is on the political economy of globalisation.[3] But that does not mean a narrowly economic view. On the contrary, an overly narrow approach by the economic profession has, in my view, not only been to the detriment of economics as a subject area, but is also culpable to a degree for the huge damage inflicted upon the international economy – and community – by the 2007–2008 global financial crash and the resulting 2009 global recession, the results of which are still being paid in many countries today through stagnating wages, high unemployment, and government austerity measures that are undermining investments in education, health and other services, and on the social and productive infrastructure. That culpability comes from economic theory having been used to justify the form and nature of free-market globalisation that led to the crash. These failures of economic theory are returned to below, once we've addressed the three questions of whether globalisation is new, so what, and what might be done about it. First, though, some context.

1.1   The current era of globalisation

Arguably, it is the globalisation of *finance* that marks out the current era of globalisation. As Perraton (2011, p. 73) argues:

---

[3] On the rather separate literature regarding globalisation and culture, see for example Pieterse (1994), Inglehart (2000), and Harvey (2009).

Particularly since the demise of the Bretton Woods system, international finance has grown exponentially to almost astronomical levels for some products. The 2008– crisis illustrated the interconnections of global financial markets as complex derivative products transmitted a crisis originating in the US sub-prime loans market across the world.

The level of transactions is extraordinary. Whereas in the early 1970s the ratio of foreign exchange trading to world trade was around 2:1, by the early 1990s this ratio had risen to 50:1 and is around 70:1 today (Eatwell and Taylor, 2000, pp. 3–4); the majority of these foreign exchange positions are held for less than a week.

However, Sutcliffe and Glyn (2011, pp. 87–88) sound a cautionary note:

It is our opinion that the degree of globalisation in this sense, as well as its novelty, has been greatly exaggerated. Consider the following two paragraphs:

1. An ever-increasing proportion of the world's production is sold outside the countries where it was produced. International trade has grown more than production in every year since 1945. And over the whole period since then foreign investment has grown even more rapidly than trade. Capitalist corporations operate increasingly in more than one country; and the value of the world-wide sales of MNCs and of their associated companies comes to more than one third of the gross product of the world. The number of MNCs has risen from 7000 in the early 1960s to more than 60,000 in the year 2000.

2. The immense majority of what is produced in the world is consumed in its country of production, as it was in 1913. This percentage may grow because services, which are traded less than goods, are increasing disproportionately. The largest MNCs now produce a lower percentage of output in the USA than they did in 1977. The value of the sales of branches of US and Japanese MNCs is growing more slowly than the world economy as a whole. No more than 12 per cent of the world's capital stock is foreign-owned; foreign investment is not much greater in relation to world output than it was in 1913.

Which of these two cameos corresponds to the real face of capitalism today? The answer is that this question is like the famous optical illusion puzzles in which one line looks longer than the other when they are really exactly the same length. Both the paragraphs are based on exactly the same body of information. They simply select and present it in a different way.

Similarly, many studies report that globalisation leads to growth and poverty reduction (see for example Dollar and Kraay, 2004; Milner and Kubota, 2005), with others questioning the empirical basis of such findings (see for example Wade, 2004; Lee and Vivarelli, 2006; Goldberg and Pavcnik, 2007), and others somewhere in between (Kose et al., 2009). Thus, Goldin and Kutarna (2016b) echo the point about viewing the same picture from different perspectives:

> Take economic development. Step back and view humanity as a whole, and the absolute story is broadly positive. The emerging global middle class – the middle third of humanity by income – have seen real incomes rise some 60% to 70% since 1988. The bottom third have seen theirs rise over 40%. But the relative view is sharply different. Rank humanity by wealth, and in 2015 the top 62 people in the world held more wealth than the bottom 3.6 billion.

> Move one step closer. Break humanity down into component countries and the picture changes once again. In aggregate, over the past quarter-century, the average income in poorer, developing countries has been catching up to the average income in richer, advanced economies – and quickly. Since 2000, the number of countries classified as 'low income' by the World Bank has halved, from more than 65 to 33. But as with people, so with states: the relative fortunes of the global top and bottom diverge widely. Since 1990, the average income in the world's 20 poorest countries has risen some 30% in real terms, from about $270 to $350 – an increase of $80. Income in the twenty richest countries has also risen about 30%, from $36,000 to $44,000 – an increase of $8,000.

> Finally, take one more step closer to peer within countries, and divergence once again dominates the picture. Within almost all countries, from the least developed to the most, the gap between rich and poor has widened over the past few decades.

> Nigeria, now Africa's biggest economy, has also become one of the world's most unequal. In the last two decades, the total income generated by Nigeria's economy has almost doubled, in real per person terms. Shockingly, so has the share of Nigerians living in poverty – from over 30% to over 60%. In the US, the top fifth have seen their real incomes rise over 25% since 1990; the bottom fifth have seen theirs fall 5%. Put another way, America's bottom fifth were earning more money back when the US economy had 40% less income per person to spread around.

For a fuller discussion of these themes, see Goldin and Kutarna (2016a). We now return to the questions of whether all this is new, whether and why it matters, and what might usefully be done about it?

1.2   Is globalisation new?

To answer the first question: what is *not* new, is change. Change has been happening since the universe was created in the Big Bang around 13.8 billion years ago, or for at least 6,000 years since God created the world, depending on whether you're a creationist or not. Either way, change has been happening for some time. So, to agree that the world is now totally different than it was previously, is not really saying very much: if you're on a week-long train journey, you might look out the window and say you're in a totally different place, so in that sense it's totally different from the day before. But then you'll say the same thing the next day; so yes, it is completely different, except that you have just said exactly the same thing as you did the previous day – that you're in a totally different place, and everything has changed.

And so it is with globalisation. Yes, by just about any measure we live in more globalised times than ever before. But then, that's what people have been saying for years and indeed generations. So, has the rate of change speeded up, or is it just the same old change as has always been trundling along?

To make sense of this question, we need to distinguish between the *quantitative* degree of globalisation – the trade-to-GDP ratio may have risen from 40 to 50 per cent, or the proportion of national residents born outside the country may have risen from 8 per cent to 10 per cent – and the *qualitative* nature of globalisation, whereby elected governments may now have less authority to implement their mandates, in face of pressures from outside the country; or the quality of life and even the continuation of the species may be threatened by global climate change.

Once broken down in this way, we can say that the degree of globalisation has been on a reasonably steady upward trajectory since – well, probably forever, but with a marked increase following the Industrial Revolution and the emergence of capitalism, with economic activity organised within profit-seeking companies where the desire to continually increase profits will tend to lead them to seek to expand their activities in all ways, including geographically, which includes across borders.

This continual drive to ever more globalisation has waxed and waned. The phenomenon of globalisation even spread to armed conflict, so the enormous increase in globalisation in the 19th century and early years of the 20th century, which included the 'scramble for Africa' between the advanced capitalist powers, led to the First World War. This in turn derailed many of the globalisation processes, most notably by impos-ing war reparations on Germany that they would be unable to meet, thus ruining their economy and guaranteeing that they could neither buy our goods nor produce many goods to sell to us, so the previous growth in international trade levels suffered as a result. Added to which, the First World War led to the Russian Revolution, with that country exiting the world capitalist scene for seventy five years or so. The 1929 Wall Street Crash and subsequent Great Depression of the 1930s was international, but it too tempered the growth of international trade.

Following the Second World War there was a conscious effort to con-struct an international system of political and economic governance that would enable a managed growth of international economic activ-ity over time, with the creation of the United Nations, the International Monetary Fund (IMF), and the World Bank, and with the restoration of the gold standard to which currency levels could be fixed, this time with gold exchangeable at a fixed price to the US dollar, rather than as had previously been the case, against the pound sterling. This inter-national economic system oversaw the longest era of sustained eco-nomic growth and development that capitalism has ever experienced, over the thirty years from 1945 to 1975 or so. There were increasing strains to the system. Most notable was the inability – or rather the political unwillingness – of the US government to pay for the costs of the Vietnam War through taxation. Instead, they paid for it by print-ing money. This led in time to President Nixon having to abandon the fixed price of dollars in terms of gold – as eventually there were too many dollars held outside the US for America to be able to honour the commitment to exchange them for the gold held at Fort Knox, on request.

There was then something of an interregnum, during which alterna-tive ways forward were advocated by political parties of the left and right across the world. With the election of Prime Minister Thatcher in the UK and President Reagan in the US, that competition of political manifestos was decided in the 1980s – in favour of promoting laissez-faire, market-based solutions; rather than renewing public institutions nationally and internationally with a view to creating a new, interventionist, architecture for recovery. With the fall of the Berlin Wall in 1989 and of the Soviet Union in 1991, free-market capitalism was given a double boost globally. First, whole swathes of the world market that had been effectively out of bounds, or at least restricted, for private firms – the Soviet Union, and then Eastern Europe – became open for business. And second, for all its faults, the Soviet Union was considered globally to represent an alternative way of organising the economy to that of capitalism, with a planned economy and no unemployment, and with free education and health-care, housing provided at low cost, and so on. There is no doubt that governments elsewhere – most particularly in Western Europe – felt obliged to match those achievements, committing themselves to maintaining full employment and a welfare state. With that alternative gone, the constraint was lifted, and Western governments could do as they pleased. This ushered in a new era, depicted by the late Andrew Glyn as 'Capitalism Unleashed'.[4]

So, the Golden Age of Capitalism[5] of 1945–1975 was replaced by an era of Capitalism Unleashed, from the 1980s. This new era saw a continued process of globalisation, but with capital rather than governments and public institutions in control. 'Capitalism unleashed' was, therefore, qualitatively different, most notably ushering in increased inequality within almost all countries, with the pay and wealth levels for those at the top ballooning, most notably the top 1 per cent – and even more strikingly, the top 0.1 per cent. These huge new fortunes have not come from collective economic success – they have been a *distributional* phenomenon, with the wealthy becoming wealthier, even when the companies and economies they have been overseeing have failed to match previous performances under the more regulated and egalitarian era. Whilst the rapid growth of China, and to a lesser extent some other developing countries, pulled hundreds of millions out of poverty over these years, thus possibly reducing inequality between individuals on a global scale,[6] inequality has *increased within* almost all

---

4 Andrew Glyn, *Capitalism Unleashed* (Oxford University Press, 2006).

5 *The Golden Age of Capitalism* was the title of a book edited by Stephen Marglin and Juliet Schor (Oxford University Press, 1991).

6 On which, see Cruz et al. (2015) and Anand and Segal (2015); Bourguignon and Morrisson (2002) document the growth over the previous two centuries in such inequality.

countries,[7] and in the richer economies this has in some cases meant that the elimination of poverty that one might have expected by now has not occurred.

This growth of inequality has had detrimental economic and social effects. At the bottom end of the spectrum, these detrimental economic and social effects include the fiscal costs of benefit and other such payments; plus the costs borne by the health and other services; as well as the potential tax revenues foregone, had those in poverty instead been in a position to pay more in tax (even the poorest will pay some tax, through sales taxes such as VAT).[8] Other costs include the failure to put pressure on companies to invest, modernise and improve efficiency, if instead they can pay low wages which make the concomitantly low productivity levels affordable. (For a discussion of the deleterious effects of low wages on productivity and economic dynamism, see Michie and Wilkinson, 1995.)

The new era also, crucially, allowed free rein to money to roam the globe without the previous restrictions that had been put in place to try to deliver a degree of stability and productive purpose. The abolition of exchange controls led to huge cross-border flows of finance. Initially this was explained as being akin to removing a dam – the water will rush, but will then establish a new equilibrium, and normal flows will be resumed. Not so. The huge speculative flows continued – driven by the fact that that's what they were – not investments, or flows to correct past distortions, but speculation. The growth of global financial speculation went hand in hand with the increased wealth of the top 1 per cent – or even more so, the top 0.1 per cent. Largely these fortunes were coming from such speculative activity – directly or indirectly. But these 'high net worth individuals' as the new super-rich liked to be referred to, then wanted new financial instruments to be created for them to hold their wealth in, to speculate and make further gains.[9] This process drove the global economy from the mid-1980s, generating a series of financial crises in different regions of the world, until it came tumbling down with the global financial crash of 2007–2008 – which the deregulated era of 'capitalism unleashed' had caused. That in turn created a

7 Indeed, it is the rise of the super-wealthy in developing countries which has reduced the disparities globally, as documented by Anand and Segal (2016).

8 Bramley et al. (2016) estimate the cost of poverty to the UK in 2016 as being £78 billion.

9 For an analysis of the role played by the super-rich in creating a demand for the new financial products, alongside the culpable financial institutions for having designed and supplied them, see Lysandrou (2011).

global recession in 2009 – the first global recession since the 1930s, with world income and output levels actually falling (rather than just rates of growth declining, or with falls in some countries but not in aggregate).

1.3   So what – does it matter?

So, that 20- or 25-year era of capitalism unleashed had marked a new phase of globalisation – namely financial globalisation, with the abolition of exchange controls and a general deregulation of banking and the 'financial services sector' generally. What UK Chancellor of the Exchequer Gordon Brown had described as 'light touch' regulation not 'soft touch' – but which turned out to be most definitely a soft touch. And with Gordon Brown in his 2006 Mansion House speech praising the assembled bankers and businesspeople for their 'leadership skills and entrepreneurship'.

The 2007–2008 global financial crash has been widely recognised as having been caused by inappropriately deregulatory policies giving the 'financial services' sector free rein to create new 'financial products', often deliberately complex so as to hide their true nature from those buying them, from the regulators, and indeed from their own Boards of Directors who often would not have had a clue what their own companies were getting up to, in order to make ever-higher – and patently unsustainable – returns from their global operations. It was also widely recognised in the aftermath of that global crash that there had to be a re-regulation; a rebalancing back towards manufacturing and away from finance; and towards a more diverse corporate sector – particularly in the financial services sector. But what has been actually delivered and achieved over these past ten years or so falls far short of what was generally acknowledged to have been required. It certainly fell far short of the complete overhaul of global economic institutions that had led to the Golden Age of Capitalism. Instead, in 2017 the global economy was still stuck in an interregnum between the 1980s–2007 era of capitalism unleashed, and whatever the next global era should be, to replace the failed experiment of a 'greed is good' free-for-all.

1.4   What might we be doing about this?

We need to create a 21st century equivalent of the 1945 Bretton Woods system. That era was based on the creation of the IMF and World Bank, with fixed exchange rates globally, combined with domestic commitments to full employment and, at least in Western Europe, welfare states. It is clear, in my view, what the next new era should look like – the problem is creating the political consensus across countries to see it developed and delivered.

We need a 'Green New Deal', along the lines of Roosevelt's New Deal that was launched in 1930s USA to tackle the Great Depression, but this time to tackle climate change, globally. This would include major public investment in green technologies, as well as in modernising and renewing the productive and social infrastructure that countries require, but in environmentally friendly ways. Indeed, we need to renew the productive and social infrastructure precisely to make it more environmentally sustainable. Supplying our energy needs through renewables requires both investment in those renewable facilities and technologies (including improved battery storage, carbon capture and so on), and a reduction in the use of energy, via investment in less energy-intensive technologies, buildings and lifestyles. More fundamentally it means refocusing away from GDP and growth, towards the quality of life and well-being.[10]

We need to re-establish control over casino capitalism's speculative financial flows, currently still sloshing across the globe in search of a quick turn. We need greater corporate diversity within countries globally, with public enterprise alongside private, and with a 'third sector' of member-ownership alongside shareholder-ownership to enable co-operatives, mutuals and employee-owned enterprises to play a greater role. Global institutions are required, to match this new agenda. Inequality needs to be tackled, with excessive levels of top 'rewards' either abolished or effectively taxed – and personal and corporate tax avoidance and evasion needs to be stopped. While all this needs to be done at the global level, so too this agenda needs to be promoted at the national level, and at sub-national regional and local levels. Indeed, to tackle climate change, the amount of needless international transportation of goods needs to be replaced by stronger local and regional communities and economies, with successful 'localism' becoming the starting point for economic and social investment and progress – rather than pursuing international agreements to give yet more power and authority to global corporations over elected governments.

10 On which, see for example Raworth (2017).

But at the time of writing (March 2017) there seems little likelihood of the above package being pursued and implemented globally, or even in many countries. More likely seems to be a continued drift, followed by a renewed era of capitalism unleashed, leading to another global crash five, ten or twenty years later, 'requiring' a further round of austerity measures, quite likely causing a further 'lost decade' of economic stagnation, social regression and political tension.

However, during the 1930s, with Hitler in power in Germany, and fascist regimes in Italy, Spain and Portugal, and a militaristic regime in Japan, plus much of the rest of the world still colonised, it would have seemed unlikely that by 1945 a new international order would have been established based on global co-operation, and domestic commitments to full employment, that would usher in the most successful era of sustained economic growth and development that capitalism had ever enjoyed. Of course, world war concentrated minds. But it should be possible for minds to become concentrated without world war, particularly as the world is rapidly approaching an arguably greater threat in the form of climate change. The next chapter therefore considers this historical context – where globalisation came from, in order to better consider in subsequent chapters where it might be heading – and what might be done to influence that direction of travel.

1.5   The failure and culpability of mainstream economics

Chapter 3 on the theory of globalisation reports on what the founders of political economy – Adam Smith, David Ricardo, and Karl Marx – said on the subject of what in their day was a still emerging system of capitalism. And about its inherent tendency to trade overseas and to expand its production across borders – key drivers behind the tendency towards globalisation, from their day to the present. Whatever happened to that approach, of political economy, that set out to analyse the fundamental forces at work in society that were driving the economy, that saw the division of wealth and income between the great social classes as being of fundamental importance in understanding the dynamics of the system, and which recognised and indeed stressed the importance of historical, institutional, cultural and political processes, as well as an appreciation of the motives of individuals that went beyond just utility maximisation for consumers, and profit maximisation for firms? The answer is, such lines of enquiry were thought dangerous, such that towards the end of the 19th century, modern-day, mainstream economics was developed and took hold, focusing on the individual as the object of analysis, rather than on social classes. This process was encouraged by the ethos of the day when it was thought that the emerging mathematical and physical sciences would be able to uncover the mysteries of the world around us, including the economy. We can see in retrospect that this goal was never going to be achieved – and never could be. The economy isn't a machine, the workings of which can be precisely calculated. As John Maynard Keynes – arguably the greatest economist broadly within the mainstream tradition – recognised and stressed, there are too many unknowns and unknowables, too much depends on consumer confidence and the 'animal spirits' of investors.[11]

One of the central failings of mainstream economics is that it tends to adopt simplifying assumptions in order to make theorising and calculations 'tractable'. This of course is a necessary part of any theorising. A one-to-one scale map is not much use. But the problem occurs when economists then fail to reintroduce all those real-world complications that have been abstracted from, when delivering policy conclusions and advice. Thus, conclusions and advice are delivered that are based on unrealistic assumptions. The reason is usually because – as was reported above as having been recognised by Keynes – reality is just too complicated to fully restore into the workings. So what should be done? First, any restrictive assumptions should be made explicit. Second, the resulting conclusions and policy advice should be caveated as most likely not being directly applicable to the real world. And third, where some sort of policy agenda does nevertheless need to be followed, the above weaknesses should be borne in mind. Thus, we should hedge our bets by promoting a rich ecosystem of alternative corporate forms – shareholder-ownership, public ownership, and member-ownership of firms, rather than assuming that the textbook model of shareholder-ownership will maximise returns to society. Similarly, when theory demonstrates that one course of action is optimal, since winners can compensate losers with everyone thereby being better off, the resulting policy shouldn't be adopted on those grounds alone, unless there is convincing evidence that the winners will indeed actually compensate the losers.

---

11 Or as the civil servant Sir Humphrey from the British TV series 'Yes Minister' put it: 'I foresee all sorts of unforeseen problems.'

This last example – from welfare economics – is crucial to the theory of trade and globalisation, as discussed in Chapter 3 below. Briefly, those who felt they had not been compensated for the costs of globalisation made their feelings known in 2016 by getting Donald Trump the Republican nomination and by voting in large numbers for Bernie Sanders to be the Democrat nominee; and in the UK, voting for Jeremy Corbyn to lead the Labour Party, and voting for the UK to leave the European Union. Similar examples have been seen globally, which have in varying degrees been ascribed to 'anti-globalisation'.

2 Globalisation in historical context

Journalist: 'What do you think of Western civilization?'
Gandhi: 'I think it would be a good idea'
(unknown source)

Several decades ago I heard a joke along the lines of there being a conference of Native Americans in New York for which the final conference dinner dress code was traditional dress; when one of the delegates in full tribal dress went to the hotel Reception to check on the room for the dinner, the receptionist gave directions and then asked 'Is this your first time in New York?', to which the Native American replied 'yes'. 'So, how do you like our city?' asked the receptionist. 'It's fine', replied the Native American, 'How do you like our country?'.

The point, of course, is that while there are today huge movements of people globally, this is not entirely new. Reference was made in the previous chapter to the years leading up to the First World War being one of globalisation, with firms from Britain, Germany and elsewhere seeking to do business abroad; with trade levels rising; and also with large movements of migrants, including from Europe to the USA.

There is also the standard joke of a Frenchman in France asking an Algerian 'Why are you here?', inviting the reply, 'Because you were there'. There was, then, migration of colonial settlers from France, Britain and the other colonial powers to administer their colonies; and after independence this has generally been followed by migration from those former colonies to the former colonial powers.

Whilst there has always been movement of people across the globe, the development of capitalism gave rise to the need for large concentrations of workers within single factories, mines and mills, and with such workplaces often being geographically clustered, thus requiring very large numbers of workers to migrate to those areas. In part this was delivered in most countries by migration from the countryside to where the employment needs were, but in many cases such domestic migration was supplemented by international migration. One ironic case in the UK was when Enoch Powell – who was to become known for his 'rivers of blood' speech warning against immigration – had previously as Health Minister encouraged a large number of immigrants from the Commonwealth (including the West Indies) into the understaffed National Health Service.

One form of globalisation that the development of capitalism certainly fostered was, then, the global movement of labour – to provide the labour-force for the factories and other workplaces. The other option, of course, was for the factories to go to the employees – and that too has happened. So globalisation has seen the growth of multinational companies, initially meaning companies establishing factories in other countries, so as to be able to hire their employees, and then increasingly operating across borders more generally, to access inputs, sell their products, and also acquire overseas companies.

Globalisation also includes increased international trade. This can be one company selling to a second company in another country, or directly to consumers in that country. It can also be a company transferring goods and components from one part of its global operation to another part of the same company in another country. This last aspect of globalisation then directly raises issues of taxation, since if a company is producing components in one country and manufacturing in another, and if the two countries have different rates of corporation tax, then the company can alter the amount of tax it pays by adjusting the price at which it sells its components to itself, so as to ensure that the profits appear in the jurisdiction with the lower tax rate. This simple example of 'transfer pricing' has of course been developed hugely by today's great tax avoiding multinational companies.

This form of globalisation – of firms operating across borders; of buying components and selling products internationally; of encouraging migration into countries where their factories are short of workers; of buying foreign firms whether to remove competition or to utilise their assets; and moving money across borders for tax avoidance, speculation or other purposes – followed on from the establishment of the capitalist firm, owned by a private individual or by shareholders, and increasingly driven by the desire to obtain a financial return on that ownership. This development arose first in Britain, through the Industrial Revolution. Britain was already a global power, with its colonies and navy, but it now became a globalising power, seeking to ensure that 'its' firms could expand and profit beyond its borders.

Once other countries followed suit – the US, France, Holland, Spain, Germany – then this gave a two-fold impetus to these pressures for globalisation: first, they too followed the above path, adding to global trade, production, migration, and financial flows; but second, they also clashed. The same companies would be competing for the same investment sites, for the same markets, for the same supplies, for the same employees, and so on. And in that competition, national governments could be relied on to support the interests of 'their' companies. Amongst other things, this led to the 'scramble for Africa', as the emerging capitalist powers secured areas for their companies to operate in, by establishing colonies. This era of globalisation ended only with the global war that it helped bring about, namely the First World War.

That was a World War, not only because the world's leading industrialised countries were involved, but also because they sought to bring their colonies into action on their side, most notably of course Britain, being the dominant colonial power – with the account of one such Australian soldier exemplified in the song 'And the Band Played Waltzing Matilda', maimed in the Battle of Gallipoli. (Some 50,000 Turks and 50,000 British, French, Australian and New Zealand troops died in the failed attempt to take the Gallipoli peninsula – a blunder due to the first Lord of the Admiralty, Winston Churchill.)

One consequence of the outbreak of war in 1914 was to help create the conditions for the Russian Revolution in 1917. This had a profound influence on the shape of globalisation processes. First, it cut Russia – and subsequently the USSR – off from such globalisation, at least in the sense that firms from the capitalist countries could not straightforwardly extend their operations into the USSR, as they could across much of the rest of the world. And second, it created the impression across the world that another way of organising the economy was possible. This meant that if capitalist globalisation fell short of what was thought might be possible through a non-capitalist route, the system itself might be inviting itself to be overthrown.

2.1   The economic consequences of the peace

Following the First World War, it might have been possible for the previous era of globalisation to have resumed, albeit with Russia having been removed from the process. Instead, the victors imposed punitive reparation payments on Germany. The economist John Maynard Keynes warned against this in *The Economic Consequences of the Peace*, in which he pointed out that such payments would prevent the German economy from recovering after the war. This would make Germany even less able to pay subsequent reparation payments. It would also leave them unable to buy goods from Britain or elsewhere. Thus, the UK economy would, ironically, be left worse off. And there would be little basis for increased trade, growth and employment.

> The future life of Europe was not their concern; its means of livelihood was not their anxiety. Their preoccupations, good and bad alike, related to frontiers and nationalities, to the balance of power, to imperial aggrandizements, to the future enfeeblement of a strong and dangerous enemy, to revenge, and to the shifting by the victors of their unbearable financial burdens on to the shoulders of the defeated. (Keynes, 1919, Chapter IV, The Treaty, paragraph IV.1)

Not for the last time, Keynes was right. His warnings proved prescient. These reparations were thus one of the reasons why there was no return to the pre-First World War era of globalisation. The Germans' inability to pay the reparations also led to them printing money to do so, which in turn created hyperinflation – which proved to be an ominous backdrop to the subsequent rise of Hitler and the Nazis to power.

> If we aim deliberately at the impoverishment of Central Europe, vengeance, I dare predict, will not limp. (Keynes, 1919, Chapter VII, Remedies, paragraph VII.1)

In Britain, Churchill had moved on from being the First Lord of the Admiralty, and despite his appalling blunder over Gallipoli, had been made Chancellor of the Exchequer. He proposed returning to the pre-First World War gold standard, whereby the pound sterling was fixed to a specific quantity of gold. Further, he proposed that this be done at the same *rate* of exchange between sterling and gold that had been in place prior to the First World War. As with Gallipoli, this too was a catastrophic blunder. Although at least this time a warning was given to that effect in advance – by John Maynard Keynes, in a pamphlet entitled *The Economic Consequences of Mr. Churchill* (Keynes, 1925). Keynes warned that such a move would make British goods uncompetitive internationally, and that the only remedy would be to cut the prices of British goods in world markets. But – and this is the key strength of Keynes over other economists – Keynes warned that economies don't behave like the economic textbooks suggest. Attempting to cut wages will not necessarily lead to a fall in the prices of the goods that those workers produce. First, the attempt to cut wages will likely fail. Second, even if they are successful, employers will not necessarily cut prices concomitantly. Third, any fall in wages will reduce consumer demand, with potentially recessionary consequences. Fourth, even if prices were to fall, this may be taken as a signal of deflationary times ahead, with damaging effects on consumer expectations and the 'animal spirits' of investors, thereby doing far more harm to the economy than good.

Churchill ignored Keynes. Britain rejoined the gold standard at the pre-First World War exchange rate of sterling for gold. British goods became uncompetitive, including for the major export, namely coal. The response was to cut the price of coal by cutting the wages of coalminers. But things didn't work like in the economic textbooks. They worked out more like Keynes had warned. The miners went on strike, leading to Britain's first and to date only general strike, in 1926.

> On grounds of social justice, no case can be made out for reducing the wages of the miners. They are the victims of the economic Juggernaut. They represent in the flesh the 'fundamental adjustments' engineered by the Treasury and the Bank of England to satisfy the impatience of the City fathers to bridge the 'moderate gap' between $4.40 and $4.86. They (and others to follow) are the 'moderate sacrifice' still necessary to ensure the stability of the gold standard. The plight of the coal miners is the first, but not – unless we are very lucky – the last, of the Economic Consequences of Mr. Churchill. (Keynes, 1925, pp. 207–230)

Thus, even the 'roaring twenties' was a mixed bag internationally. Whilst the German economy had been prevented from recovering by the imposition of the reparations payments, and the UK economy had been prevented from recovery by the decision to rejoin the gold standard at an uncompetitive rate, the US stock exchange soared. But that turned out to be unsustainable, ending in 1929 with the Wall Street Crash and the subsequent Great Depression – depicted graphically by John Steinbeck in his 1939 novel, *Grapes of Wrath*.

In 1936, at the height of the Great Depression globally, Keynes published his *General Theory of Employment, Interest and Money*, which argued that capitalism was not a self-righting system, and that it would not necessarily of its own accord return to a full employment equilibrium – which up until then, mainstream economics, and the Treasury, believed. Indeed, they still do, despite Keynes's book having demonstrated the opposite eighty years ago. In the US, Roosevelt's New Deal was very much in the spirit of Keynes's policy advice, of public work programmes to create jobs and incomes, and hence demand, which would feed through to the rest of the economy.

In Europe, General Franco attempted to overthrow Spain's elected government, sparking the 1936–1939 Spanish Civil War, but with Hitler and Mussolini supporting the fascists, and the British government refusing to support the democratically-elected Spanish government, Spain fell to fascism, and Hitler went on to occupy the Sudetenland and then Poland – sparking the Second World War.

So, ultimately the economic consequences of the peace were, as Keynes had warned, a bankrupted Germany, which following hyper-inflation and economic depression, turned to Hitler and the Nazis, leading to the Second World War. In terms of the global context of globalisation, whilst the pre-First World War era had indeed been one of increased trade and business expanding over borders, the subsequent thirty years or so, of 1914–1945 saw a continuation of business attempting to sell overseas and even to establish factories abroad, but conditions were no longer so conducive. However, in 1935, the US auto firm General Motors did build a factory in Germany to produce the 'Blitz' truck, used by the Nazis for their blitzkrieg attacks on Poland, France and the Soviet Union. Indeed, it has been said that Hitler would never have considered invading Poland without the synthetic fuel technology provided by GM. Inevitably, GM's factories in Germany were hit during allied bombing raids, although not enough to prevent them (and the Ford factories) from continuing to supply the German army. Following the war, the US government paid General Motors $32 million in compensation, for damage done to their plants in Nazi Germany.[1]

---

1 *Washington Post*, 1998, accessed from washingtonpost.com on 28 July 2016.

2.2   The Golden Age of capitalism

During the Second World War the allies planned for the post-war aftermath, and this time Keynes was not completely ignored (although as we shall see, the post-war arrangements would have been better, had his advice been followed more fully). There was a conscious effort to construct international institutions whose purpose would be to encourage international collaboration, growth and development. The institutions would include the United Nations, the International Monetary Fund (IMF), and the World Bank. The arrangements would include fixed exchange rates between all currencies, underpinned by a return to the gold standard, but this time with gold pegged to the US dollar, rather than to the pound sterling. Crucially, there would be controls on the movement of capital internationally. The aim was to restrict the movement of money globally to that necessary for genuine economic reasons – tourism, financing trade, investing in factories and other productive facilities in other countries, and so on; but to limit it at that. In other words, not to permit the transfer of funds across borders for purely speculative purposes.

All this was discussed at Bretton Woods in the US, hence the post-war international arrangements being referred to as the Bretton Woods set-up. Alongside these international arrangements went a commitment to avoid returning to the '1930s era' of mass unemployment. As Khan (2015) wrote in relation to US and other troops based during the Second World War in India, the intention was 'not only to defeat fascism, but to construct a new world order' (p. 269).[2] Such a commitment to full employment seemed practicable, as it was generally accepted that Keynes's *General Theory* had explained both the causes of unemployment and the concomitant policy cures.

National governments were committed to maintaining full employment – along with varying degrees of other welfare state provision, including housing, education, and health services. International arrangements and institutions had been established to seek similar outcomes internationally. Combined, this helped deliver what turned out to be the most successful era of sustained economic growth and development that capitalism had ever enjoyed, from 1945 through to the mid-1970s.

---

2 Adding that 'Those Americans who supported a people's war. . . looked to Gandhi and the Indian nationalists with admiration and sympathy.'

This approach was abandoned from the 1980s onwards, with a turn to privatisation, deregulation, and free capital flows; the economic (and social) outcomes have been worse. That 'Golden Age' has not as yet been repeated or matched.

Keynes led the UK delegation during the Bretton Woods negotiations. However, he would have preferred the new international arrangements to have been more 'Keynesian', with a more robust ability to maintain full employment when the system came under strain. He proposed that this be done by putting the onus in such circumstances on the 'surplus' economies (those with a Balance of Payments surplus, exporting more than they import) to take action, namely to expand their economies, which would result in their citizens and companies buying more from abroad, thus helping the other countries to pull out of recession and return to full employment. In other words, he wanted the onus to be on the rich countries to have to act. Which meant America. (Although subsequently it would have meant Germany, Japan, and other surplus countries.) America resisted, and proposed the exact opposite: that if and when the world economy got into difficulties, with unemployment emerging along with trade imbalances, it should be the deficit economies that should be forced to act, by deflating their economies, so that their people could afford to buy less, meaning that those countries would import less, thereby rectifying their balance of payments deficit. In other words, austerity.[3]

When Keynes was informed that this is what the Americans would propose, and that the British delegation would go along with it, he responded: 'So because they won't listen to sense, you propose to talk nonsense?' Thus, while Keynes had helped craft the most successful era of globalisation – what might be termed 'managed globalisation', with full employment and economic development as explicit objectives – the failure to incorporate Keynes's ideas for making it durable meant that when it did indeed come under strain, in the 1970s, it began to unravel. It was thus vulnerable to being replaced in the 1980s by the anti-Keynesian 'monetarists', and by the Thatcher and Reagan era of privatisation, deregulation, and speculative financial flows, that has been dubbed 'capitalism unleashed'.

---

3 For a discussion of the respective UK and US proposals at Bretton Woods, see also Amato and Fantacci (2014).

2.3   The breakdown of the Golden Age

The reasons for the 'Golden Age' era of globalisation breaking down have been analysed elsewhere – see for example Marglin and Schor (1992). One reason was the failure to have developed the institutional arrangements along the lines that Keynes advocated, as referred to above, rather than, as occurred, along the lines that the USA dictated – which were in the interests of their economy, rather than being in the interests of creating a sustainable international system. It is also worth noting that the economist who had developed similar ideas to Keynes during the 1930s independently, the Polish Marxist Michal Kalecki, had warned in 1943 that if the sort of policies which both he and Keynes had developed for the maintenance of full employment were implemented:

> [A] strong opposition of 'business leaders' is likely to be encountered. Lasting full employment is not at all to their liking. The workers would 'get out of hand' and the 'captains of industry' would be anxious to 'teach them a lesson'. In this situation a powerful bloc is likely to be formed between big business and the *rentier* interests, and they would probably find more than one economist to declare that the situation was manifestly unsound. The pressure of all these forces, and in particular of big business would most probably induce the Government to return to the orthodox policy of cutting down the budget deficit. A slump would follow. (Kalecki, 1943, p. 144)

And so it proved. The 'more than one economist' consisted primarily of Milton Friedman, the guru of anti-Keynesian monetarism, and advisor to Margaret Thatcher, Ronald Reagan, and General Pinochet.[4]

> One of the first acts of the Thatcher government in 1979 had been to abolish exchange controls. Up until this point, the transfer of currencies internationally was regulated, other than the US dollar that was tied to gold. This all changed from 1979, with other countries following the UK's lead, and a huge rise in capital and currency movements developing globally. This triggered what has been generally referred to as an era of globalisation, with a huge increase in the global movement of money, but also of trade, investments, and other economic activity, and also social, political, cultural and technological developments which all chimed with the idea of a new 'global village', where the 'world is flat' (Friedman, 2005).

---

4 For a critique of Milton Friedman's approach to economics, see Blackford (2016). Note that this is a different Friedman to the one cited in the following paragraph.

The extent and nature of this era of globalisation has been usefully analysed by a range of social scientists and economists. Following his tenure as Chief Economist at the World Bank, Stiglitz published a skeptical analysis of the form and nature of the free-market variant of globalisation policies that had been advocated by the 'Washington Consensus' of the International Monetary Fund and the World Bank (Stiglitz, 2002). Ha-Joon Chang questioned whether it was right to say that free-market approaches should be adopted by all, when the currently rich countries had only achieved that status through active government-sponsored industrial policies, generally protected behind exchange controls and import controls (Chang, 2002).

But the laissez-faire model of globalisation continued. Keynes had warned of the risks of such an approach at both the national and international levels. 'When the capital development of a country becomes a by-product of a casino, the job is likely to be ill-done', he had concluded in the *General Theory*, having described how stock exchange behavior could come to be driven not by economic fundamentals but by the expectations of traders as to the likely trades of the other participants, who in turn were betting on the expected behavior of others. Expectations can thus become self-fulfilling prophesies. While Keynes's stress on the importance of expectations, risk and uncertainty in the way economies operate were rather underplayed in the decades leading up to the 2007–2008 global financial crisis, the question of risk was sometimes referred to, but only within the damagingly complacent context of the claim that risks had been dealt with, it was suggested, as these had been insured against, including via innovative new financial products. (Michie, 2015, pp. 98–99)

And as Monbiot (2016) put it, in his analysis of neoliberalism:

After Margaret Thatcher and Ronald Reagan took power, the rest of the package soon followed: massive tax cuts for the rich, the crushing of trade unions, deregulation, privatisation, outsourcing and competition in public services. Through the IMF, the World Bank, the Maastricht treaty and the World Trade Organization, neoliberal policies were imposed – often without democratic consent – on much of the world. Most remarkable was its adoption among parties that once belonged to the left: Labour and the Democrats, for example. As Stedman Jones notes, 'it is hard to think of another utopia to have been as fully realized'.

Thus:

> Deregulation of the financial sector was yet another big idea that was sup-
> posed to be good for Americans, and it was – for the elite. Begun in earnest
> by Reagan, the process was continued under Clinton who declared many of
> the FDR-era laws 'antiquated'. He abolished the Glass–Steagall Act, which
> kept commercial banks from speculating on Wall Street with other people's
> money. The act was supposed to be a 'major achievement that will benefit
> American consumers, communities and businesses of all sizes'. With amaz-
> ing shortsightedness, Clinton declared at the signing ceremony that we're
> 'modernizing the financial services industry, tearing down these antiquated
> walls'.
>
> Deregulation was in full swing – always framed as modernization or in the
> name of efficiency. The prohibition on interstate banking was also removed,
> allowing for the creation of 'too big to fail' banks. In 2000, Congress
> passed the Commodity Futures Modernization Act, which prohibited the
> regulation of credit default swaps. (Komlos, 2016)

2.4   Capitalism unleashed

The era of 'capitalism unleashed' has in some ways been a return to
the pre-First World War era of globalisation: with the fall of the Soviet
Union, and the opening of China to trade and investment, practically
the whole globe is once again up for grabs when multinational companies scour the horizon for opportunities; there has been a return to a
single dominant power (then Britain, now America) relatively untram-
meled by international agreements and regulation; and military force,
including invasion and occupation, has once again become a more
natural part of the picture. But there are of course big differences:
America is not as dominant as Britain had been, nor even as dominant as it itself was previously – the world economy now has several
large economies, none strong enough to, for example, underpin the
world financial system on their own. Co-operation is actually more
necessary than ever. And most crucially, in terms of what's different in
today's era, we now face the threat of climate change – which must be
tackled, which can be done only through concerted action by national
governments, acting together.

The era of capitalism unleashed, since the 1980s, has generally been
referred to as one of neoliberalism, recognising the echoes with

the pre-First World War era of laissez-faire economic liberalism. The Golden Age had been delivered in European countries through state ownership of much of the productive infrastructure: water, electricity, gas, roads, rail, and so on. Much of this was handed back to the private sector through privatisation programmes. And while the Golden Age had been based on the control of speculative financial flows across borders, the 'free movement of capital' was given free rein. Economic growth has generally been lower under this era of globalisation. However, the development of China in particular, but also elsewhere, has seen hundreds of millions raised out of poverty. This has been a welcome and significant development. Of course, it might well have occurred had the Golden Age continued. And in terms of laissez-faire, it should be noted that China has actually continued with widespread state ownership of much of the productive infrastructure, and indeed more widely, with many state-owned enterprises.

Along with low growth, but a global move out of poverty, the other two main characteristics of the current era of globalisation – leaving aside climate change – has been a huge growth of inequality within most countries, and increased economic instability, domestically and globally.

The growth in inequality has been documented amongst others by Piketty (2014). Whilst within countries such as Britain, the growth of home ownership provides a form of wealth to many in the population who previously would have had little, this is an effect amongst the working and middle classes. The growth in inequality has been in the increased share of income and wealth going to the very richest – the 1 per cent. This is reflected in huge increases in executive pay compared to what the average employee in that executive's company receives. And because this has taken place in an era of neoliberalism or laissez-faire, taxation on high incomes and levels of wealth has actually fallen, at precisely the time when it is most needed. Campbell and Lusher (2016), looking at US data, agree with Piketty that while there have been many factors contributing to the growth of inequality since the Reagan era, the key one was the cuts in top marginal tax rates.

It might be asked whether this matters – this growth in inequality, with the very rich pulling away from the rest of society in this way? The architect of 'New Labour' in Britain, that led to Tony Blair being elected and re-elected as Prime Minister, famously said that he was 'intensely relaxed' about the rich getting richer (although he has since gone on record as recognising that this attitude was mistaken).

But it does have damaging consequences, economically, socially and politically. Many of these damaging consequences have been documented by Richard Wilkinson and Kate Pickett in *The Spirit Level: Why More Equal Societies Almost Always Do Better* (2009). As referred to in the introductory chapter, increased inequality also led globally to a new appetite from the very wealthy for the creation of new economic instruments for them to invest and speculate in, which fuelled the speculate bubble that led to the 2007–2008 global financial crisis and subsequent global recession and consequent austerity measures.

2.5   Conclusion: eras of globalisation

It is often said that today's world is totally transformed from the one we lived in only a few years ago, and that the pace of change is accelerating, with big data, new means of communication, and innovative technologies. Certainly, things change and everything's different. And we live in a more globalised world. But globalisation isn't new. This 'ever changing world in which we live in' was commented upon some time ago.[5] We've seen almost all of it before: new technologies, including communications and transportational; growth in trade; global companies; mass migration; even world wars.[6]

Thus, the US and the UK, who now preach the free-market 'capitalism unleashed' form of globalisation to the world as being the appropriate form for economic development, themselves achieved their development *via* a rather different route, behind tariff barriers, with public support to their industries, with international capital flows firmly under their control, and with their governments on hand to support 'their' firms globally, including through the use of 'gunboat diplomacy' and other such measures. In a sustained critique along these lines, Chang (2011) puts it thus:

> If the policies and institutions that the rich countries are recommending to the poor countries are not the ones that they themselves used when they were developing, what is going on? We can only conclude that, whether

---

5   Paul McCartney and Linda McCartney (1973), theme song for James Bond film of the same name, 'Live and Let Die'.

6   For a detailed analysis of the forces of globalisation and technological change, and the impact of these forces over the centuries, see Milanovic (2016), and for an alternative view of globalisation in historical perspective, see Goldin and Kutarna (2016a).

intentionally or not, the rich countries are effectively 'kicking away the ladder' that allowed them to climb to where they are now.

It is no coincidence that economic development has become more difficult during the last two decades, when the developed countries have been turning up the pressure on the developing countries to adopt the so-called 'good' policies and institutions. Their average annual per capita income growth rate has been halved (from 3 per cent to 1.5 per cent) between the 1960–80 period and the 1980–2000 period. And even this disappointing growth rate would not have been achieved except for rapid growth in large countries like China and India, which have not followed the orthodox strategy but have reformed and opened up their economies at their own pace. During this period, Latin America has virtually stopped growing, while sub-Saharan Africa and most ex-Communist countries have experienced a fall in absolute income. Economic instability has increased markedly, as manifested in the dozens of financial crises we have witnessed over the last decade alone. Income inequality has been growing in many developing countries and poverty has increased, rather than decreased, in a significant number of them. (Chang, 2011, p. 472)

Thus, what is new is not the *fact* of globalisation, but its *form*. Instead of the 'managed' or 'controlled' globalisation in place during the more successful Golden Age of Capitalism (1945–1975), we have the neoliberal free-for-all of capitalism unleashed (1980–today), with privatisation, deregulation, monetisation, tax cuts for corporations and the wealthy, a weakening of trade unions, and a deliberate transfer of power from governments to corporations having led to increased inequality, the creation of a super-wealthy elite, and increased instability. And having led to the global financial crisis of 2007–2008 and the global recession of 2009, followed by austerity-induced stagnation across much of the world. A lost decade. So when people say that 'globalisation is a fact', that you 'can't roll back globalisation', and so on, this misses the key question of what form and type of globalisation we choose, and what sort we want.[7]

The question is, then, what *should* be done about all this? But before we get on to that, we should delve a little deeper into the theory of globalisation: what are the causal factors and mechanisms involved, what are its impacts, and what are the possible and likely future trajectories?

---

7 For example, Tony Blair: 'I hear people say we have to stop and debate globalisation. You might as well debate whether autumn should follow summer.' 2005 Labour Party Conference.

3   The theory of globalisation

> On my first day as a graduate student in economics at the Massachusetts
> Institute of Technology, the professor introduced the discipline by inton-
> ing, 'All of economics is a subset of the theory of separating hyperplanes.'
> (You don't want to know what the mathematical term means.) I started
> to giggle. But then I looked around. Everyone else was scribbling notes.
> So I wiped the smirk off my face and muttered, only to myself, that I
> had thought economics was about the plight of people living in sub-
> Saharan Africa, of the impact of technological change on living standards.
> Apparently I thought wrong – and wondered whether I had made a terrible
> career choice.
> (Michael M. Weinstein, *New York Times*, 18 September 1999)

What causes globalisation? One aspect of globalisation is migration,
and if our species first originated in what is now Africa, then clearly our
ancestors must have migrated globally, presumably in search of food.
More recently, global trade features in Shakespeare's 'The Merchant
of Venice', about a 16th century merchant involved in international
trade;[1] and the 19th century opium wars were fought between Britain
and China not only over the opium trade, but trade rights more generally (although the British also gained Hong Kong – at least for a while).
Economic forces are clearly important.

3.1   Smith, Ricardo, Marx

Adam Smith's *Wealth of Nations* (1776) is often thought to be the
first comprehensive and systematic analysis of the economy, and of
economics – indeed, helping to found the discipline of economics,

---

1 On Shakespeare, see and listen to the free podcasts by Professor Emma Smith including on The
Merchant of Venice (2012); (her 2016 BBC Radio 3 talk included the great line: Shakespeare
walked into a bar, and the barman asked 'Why the long plays?'), retrieved on 12 January 2017 from
https://podcasts.ox.ac.uk/merchant-venice-0.

or political economy which is what it was referred to then, and for a reason, as Adam Smith and his contemporaries, as well as subsequent economists, recognised the importance of institutions and political processes in economic life. Indeed, what Adam Smith was analysing was an emerging new economic, social and political system, of capitalism, that would come to not only replace feudalism in Britain, but would dominate the world. So Adam Smith was inevitably interested in analysing the division of the capitalist system between its classes: the emerging capitalist class, and the working class that it was creating. He was interested in the division of wealth between these classes, along with the old aristocracy, as being central to the dynamics of the economy – and society – as a whole. One of his key arguments was that the division of labour enabled an increase in productivity, and that the growth of the market facilitated that process, just as increased productivity and the concomitant fall in prices would help companies to expand into new markets. Hence, growth and dynamism were at the heart of his analysis and thinking. This links to globalisation, as when such developments have progressed to the extent that they are being constrained by national borders, there will be pressure to operate across and beyond those borders, so as to extend the market still further, to enjoy still greater division of labour and increased productivity.

One of the next great founders of the discipline was David Ricardo (1772–1823). He is perhaps best known for his contribution to the 'theory of comparative advantage', which could be thought of as a justification of – and indeed a call for – increased trade, including internationally. His argument is that even if your country is better at producing everything than another country, it will still be in your interest to concentrate on producing the goods that you are *much* better at – *comparatively* better. Sell those to the other country, stop producing things that you are only slightly better at, so as to concentrate all your resources on the things you are much better at, and buy the rest from the other country. He demonstrated that as a result of this trade – enabling both countries to concentrate on the things on which they had a comparative advantage – more would be produced in total, so both would end up being better off.

Marx (1818–1883) developed the ideas of Smith and Ricardo in various ways. Crucially for the issue of globalisation, he saw the capitalist firms as having an inexorable tendency to expand, to create new value, over and above what was required just to pay the workers and for the other inputs into the process, and to plough that surplus back, expanding still further. Part of this tendency to expand was to win the competition against rival firms – or to at least survive in the face of such competition. So again, when such expansion comes up against national borders, the pressure will be to go beyond them, and to continue expanding globally. Hence the development of multinational companies. And of imperialism, as such companies call on 'their' governments to protect and promote their interests as against companies from other countries.

But Marx saw capital not just as 'self-expanding value' (meaning the above process, of having to create new value, or surplus value, which was the source of profits) but also as a social relation, rather than just a thing. In this sense, capital was the process of workers having no means of subsistence other than to be employed by capital, in return for which the capitalist would have power over the work process, ensuring that surplus value was created, over and above the value of the inputs, including the wages. So to operate, a capitalist firm has to have access to workers to employ. That is not as straightforward as it might sound, since it is not clear where these would come from, since if they had no other means of survival, then how could they be there, in the absence of the capitalist having arrived? The answer is that before the capitalist enterprises appeared, the population had been subsisting through feudal arrangements, working for the feudal lords as well as on their own plots (or entirely on their plots, in which case some of the produce of which would be taken by the feudal lords). So with the Industrial Revolution in Britain, these feudal serfs had to be transformed into proletarians, working for wages in the new capitalist mills, mines and factories. One example of how this occurred was the highland clearances in Scotland, where in the 18th and 19th centuries tenant farmers were cleared from the land, and the enclosures in England, where small holders were forced to leave common lands, and became available to work in the mines, mills and factories; indeed, they now had little choice. (And even those who stayed on the land were increasingly obliged to become wage labourers for emerging capitalist farmers.)

The fact that capital is a social relation – between capitalists and workers – means that the globalisation process is not straightforward, since a British capitalist in Marx's time could not simply establish a factory in another country and expect people to turn up wanting work, as the process of creating a working class, with no other means of subsistence than to work for a capitalist, had not yet occurred. They would still be subsisting on the land, or from small-scale craftwork and suchlike (the 'gig economy' of their day). Indeed, in his work *Capital* (Volume 1, 1867), he used this point to illustrate his argument about capital being a social relation, by describing just such attempts, of capitalists seeking to globalise, but discovering that no-one wished to work for them. To drive his point home, he even described the case of one British capitalist, who had half-learned the lesson, and had thus taken with him a shipload of workers to Australia. But when they arrived, they chose not to work in the factory, so the capitalist was still bereft of any workers. The unhappy capitalist, Marx argued, hadn't realised that while these individuals in Britain were workers (proletarians, with no means of subsistence other than to work for a capitalist), in Australia they were not, as the social and political process of creating a working class had not yet occurred.

This means that the process of globalisation had to include bringing about such transformations in those countries where capital wished to operate (to employ labour to make profits). So, the process of globalisation – at least in its 19th-century onwards incarnations – has been the product of the Industrial Revolution and the development of capitalism, and of that social system extending across the globe.

We have seen in the previous chapter that this process has passed through four broad historical phases to date, with the current era of uncertainty poised to go in either direction, of continuing the pre-First World War and 'capitalism unleashed' eras of laissez-faire, inequality and instability, or attempting to develop a new golden age of capitalism, this time prioritising the tackling of climate change and the creation of environmentally and socially sustainable economic growth and development. Thus, we might characterise the eras of globalisation as follows:

Pre-First World War: globalisation with Britain as the dominant power, with the international monetary system based on the gold standard fixed to the pound sterling, huge increases in global trade, multinational corporations investment and other activities, and migration, leading to the 'scramble for Africa', and ultimately the First World War.[2]

---

2 For an analysis of the pre-First World War era of globalisation as compared to the post-1960 variants, see Baldwin and Martin (1999) who draw out both the similarities (aggregate trade and capital flow ratios, and the importance of reductions in barriers to international transactions)

First World War to Second World War: failure of Germany to recover economically after the First World War, Russia taken out of the world capitalist order by the Russian Revolution, America suffering the 1929 Wall Street Crash; 1930s Great Depression; fascism in power in Germany, Italy, Spain and Portugal; attempt by Churchill to re-establish the gold standard. No great growth of globalisation, despite some international trade, migration and investments (including by GM and Ford in Germany to help arm the Nazis).

1945–1975: Golden Age of Capitalism – stable international monetary system re-established with fixed exchange rates linked to the US dollar that was convertible to gold; the United Nations, International Monetary Fund (IMF) and World Bank established; domestic commitment to full employment, and in most European countries commitments to a welfare state providing housing, health, and education, and governments playing a major role in the economy, including through public ownership of the major utilities: water, gas, electricity; and transportation: roads and railways (and often airlines and shipping). Steady growth in most aspects of globalisation, but with finance kept on a firm leash.

1975–1985: an interregnum of around a decade, whilst right and left debated whether the economic difficulties should be tackled by renewing the golden age arrangements in a more Keynesian and interventionist direction, with a new international economic order securing, amongst other things, more stability in raw material prices (something Keynes had wanted), and domestically various ideas for more public ownership and planning, including in Sweden the idea of 'wage earner funds', with a proportion of company profits going to buy shares to be controlled by the employees; or rather, moving in the opposite, monetarist direction of laissez-faire. With the election of Thatcher and Reagan, the latter prevailed.

1985–2008: 20–25 years of neoliberal, laissez-faire policies of deregulation and privatisation, most crucially letting finance off its leash, to move across the globe at will in search of any short-term speculative gain, before racing off in search of the next one. (For an analysis and discussion of neoliberalism, and its political project, see Mirowski, 2014.)

---

and differences (primarily the impact that these reductions had on trade in goods versus trade in ideas). Ruggie (1982) also discusses these eras, but from the point of view of alternative 'international economic regimes' (see for example Ruggie, 1982, p. 392).

This was an era of instability and repeated financial and economic crises across the world, culminating in the 2007–2008 global financial crash, causing a global recession in 2009 – the first time this had occurred since the 1930s.

2008–2017: so far, a nine year interregnum, where the UK electorate voted in 2016 to leave the European Union to 'take back control'; refugee migration at unprecedented levels as the Middle East continues to suffer the aftermath of the US/UK invasions of Afghanistan and Iraq and destabilisation of Libya; inequality of income and wealth continues to rise; and the promised reforms of the banking system following the crash remain far short of what would be needed to usher in a new era of stable globalisation.

3.2   The political economy of trade

As referred to above, the traditional argument in favour of free trade has, since the days of David Ricardo, been that it enables countries to specialise in the production of goods and services in which they have a comparative advantage. However, this standard case for free trade is based on a number of assumptions and simplifications:

> First, much of the literature ignores the macroeconomic context. Second, each economy is assumed to be small and open and therefore unable to affect relative prices internationally. Third, production is assumed to operate with constant or diminishing returns to scale. And fourth, the economy is assumed to be always at full employment, by definition, and with no other distortions in the economic system. (Kitson and Michie, 1995, p.633)

There have, Kitson and Michie (1995) go on to describe, been various attempts to revise orthodox trade theory: Mundell (1961) and others have considered the macroeconomic context of tariff policy and exchange rate regimes; the ability to affect world prices has been analysed in the optimum tariff literature; and the role of increasing returns has been incorporated within the so-called 'new trade theory'. Building on these and other developments in economics, it can be seen that active trade policies may usefully be used to improve outcomes, including through improved regulation of financial institutions. Thus, writing even before the 2007–2008 financial crisis, Kitson and Michie (2000, p.42) argue that:

The dangers of unfettered and ill-informed speculative activities by many financial institutions has been illustrated in the recent crises in Asia and elsewhere. A new framework will require better information, tightening up the capital backing required by banks and security houses, and greater international coordination of regulating functions.

However, Kitson and Michie (1995, pp. 649, 650) conclude that the possibility of such an approach (regulating finance, and using active trade policies to assist economies in recession to expand out of recession) 'appears ... to be unlikely'. In the absence of such a global growth strategy, they argue that the alternatives are to adopt expansionary policies at the regional or national level, and that while the limits which globalisation places on national policies have increased, this should not undermine the case for national initiatives – 'indeed, it may be that the optimal level of intervention, to expand demand and regulate capital and product markets, is higher. . . . Thus, governments should beware of the indiscriminate liberalisation of trade and international monetary arrangements.'

3.3   Regional blocks and currency unions

In addition to nation states and global institutions, we have regional blocks of nations, most prominently the European Union (EU) and the North American Free Trade Area (NAFTA). The theory is straight-forward enough: to promote economic co-operation between neigh-bouring states, and to enable them to carry more weight collectively in global economic negotiations and other arrangements. Thus, the creation of such blocks represents both a reaction to globalisation, and an attempt to shape it.[3]

Economic theory enters most explicitly in terms of creating a single currency, as the EU has done with the euro. Here there is an academic literature on 'optimum currency areas', which identifies the factors required for such a single currency to make economic sense. I have argued, in print, since before the launch of the euro that it had been badly designed, that it did not fulfil the requirements of an optimum currency area, and despite all the hype and the denials, it was actually

---

3 Hirst and Thompson (1992, 2011) argue that what we have witnessed is not so much the creation of a 'global economy', as the formation of trading blocs and national economic management restructuring.

likely to fail, certainly in the sense of damaging the economies that participated, in particular those running current account [trade] deficits with the other members, and also more fundamentally to sooner or later fall apart, as countries abandoned the single currency, even if no exit arrangements had been made.

These arguments are set out in detail in, for example, Michie (1998), but briefly, for an optimum currency area – that is, an area for which it might make sense to adopt a single currency – one either has to be sure that there won't be trade imbalances between the countries within the single currency area, or if there are to be such imbalances, then they need to be counteracted with fiscal transfers. The former, to avoid such imbalances, could be pursued through active industrial, innovation, educational and regional policies. The latter requires a common fiscal policy to match the common currency area. To achieve all this, certainly in an area such as the EU where the scale of the tasks is large, would most likely require political union. In other words, monetary union might make sense following successful political union, with a single fiscal area that creates automatic stabilisers that operate across the area – between those parts moving into trade surplus and those moving into trade deficit – along with common industrial and regional policies.

These conditions were not met, and it was therefore inevitable that when economic conditions diverged, great strain would be put on the system as a whole. That was certainly the case in 2010 when the 2007–2008 global financial crisis and subsequent 2009 global recession spilled over into the sovereign debt crises in Europe, with Greece paying the highest price in terms of the economic adjustment programmes forced upon it by the EU institutions along with the International Monetary Fund.

In July 2016 the watchdog of the International Monetary Fund (IMF), its Independent Evaluation Office, concluded that the IMF's top staff had been 'euphoric cheerleaders for the euro project', and that 'The IMF remained upbeat about the soundness of the European banking system... this lapse was largely due to the IMF's readiness to take the reassurances of national and euro area authorities at face value' (Independent Evaluation Office of the IMF, 2016). The report describes – or, I would say, recognises – that the IMF's whole approach to the Eurozone had been characterised by 'groupthink' and intellectual capture: 'Before the launch of the euro, the IMF's public statements tended to emphasize the advantages of the common currency'.[4]

But it was not just the IMF that was prone to this pro-single currency groupthink: at the time of its launch, the consensus across institutions and indeed academia was subservient to precisely the same groupthink. Those of us who at the time were pointing out that the emperor had no clothes were generally regarded as promoting a fringe view.

When Greece suffered its sovereign debt crisis, following the 2007–2008 global financial crisis and 2009 global recession, the policies of the EU and the IMF were focused not so much on the situation of and prospects for the Greek economy, as on saving the political project that was the euro. The above report from the IMF's Independent Evaluation Office recognises as much, that the true motive of EU–IMF policy had been to protect monetary union, and yet the cost of that policy – a huge fiscal squeeze which reduced national income and created an unemployment rate of 25 per cent – fell on the Greek people: 'If preventing international contagion was an essential concern, the cost of its prevention should have been borne – at least in part – by the international community as the prime beneficiary' (Independent Evaluation Office of the IMF, 2016).

I made these warnings on the eve of the launch of the euro: that Europe should not embark on their single currency project until and unless they had put the other economic and political policies, institutions and arrangements in place – in order to enable the area to operate successfully with a single currency. These warnings were ignored:

> A single currency could only be considered acceptable within an EU-wide taxation and benefit system, and with massively expanded regional transfers from rich to poor parts of the Union to ensure real economic convergence, with living standards and employment levels moving closer together throughout the Union rather than further apart. The sort of substantial increase in regional policy spending required was ruled out by the December 1992 Edinburgh Summit, and any suggestions that there should be an EU-wide tax and benefit system has been totally rejected whenever the subject has been raised. There seems no prospect that the richer countries are prepared to see very substantial income transfers to poorer regions

---

4 See 'IMF admits disastrous love affair with the euro, apologises for the immolation of Greece', *The Telegraph*, 29 July 2016.

either in the form of regional policy or through the automatic transfers of a tax and benefit system. . . .

The power of international capitalism to dictate to nationally elected governments is not new, although it is true that it has been boosted in recent years by the free-market, deregulatory policies pursued by governments. Probably the clearest example of such a process, designed to increase the power of multinational capital and financial markets, has been the programme of increased European Community/Union integration. It is quite wrong to interpret this process as a reaction to the increased power of multinational capital; on the contrary, the Single European Market programme and now the Maastricht proposals for a single currency have themselves deliberately shifted the balance away from governments. To respond effectively to the challenges of growth, employment, social policy and so on will require the exact opposite of everything that the Maastricht treaty represents – which is a return to the laissez-faire politics of the 1920s where any suggestion that governments could act was opposed by the Treasury using the very same arguments as now (that reflation in one country is impossible, and so on).

EMU is at heart a political process which will prevent governments – whether at national or EU level – from pursuing policies to promote economic and social welfare. Such a scenario is no more sustainable now than when it was last in place, namely in the 1920s and 1930s. It is likely to come to the same unpleasant end, with individual countries being eventually forced to take action regardless of the power of international capitalism. But with the European political elite so wedded to the laissez-faire politics of Maastricht, any such attempt by the population to insist that they should be allowed to express political preferences risks taking ugly nationalist forms, against the 'internationalism' of the European central bankers and the entire existing political elite. (Michie, 1998, pp. 48, 53–54)[5]

These warnings have unfortunately been proved right, as set out in detail by, for example, Stiglitz (2016a), who refers to the 52 per cent of UK voters who voted in 2016 to leave the EU as having rebelled against 'the neoliberal agenda of the last third of the century . . . shaped by corporate and financial interests' that in effect condemned the working class in Europe and America to 'virtually no growth in their incomes in a span of two decades.' Stiglitz adds that 'Hopefully, the Brexit referendum will be a wake-up call to the EU's leaders: unless they make the EU more democratic, more democratically accountable, and more

---

5 Similar warnings were made by, for example, Arestis and Sawyer (2011).

economically successful, the likelihood of further integration, political or economic, could be nil.'[6]

3.4   Kicking away the ladder

Another area of economic – and political – theory relevant to globalisation relates to the economic policy agendas that were pursued by the industrialised countries on the one hand, and the economic policy agenda that such countries now promote for the global economy on the other. Briefly, the early industrialisers developed behind trade barriers, usually with restrictions on capital flows, and generally with public ownership or regulation of much of the productive infrastructure. Once an economy achieves a dominant position – or at least a comparatively strong one – it tends to advocate the opposite, of free trade and deregulation, since by then a level playing field will be in their interests.

This process is documented in detail by Ha-Joon Chang (2002, 2011), who argues that:

---

6   Ironically, Aldrick (2016) argues that 'The claim is simply not true' that a belief in free-markets was the ideological edifice on which the euro was built, citing as his evidence that 'The architect of the single market, which set Europe on course for the euro, was Jacques Delors, a French socialist', whereas of course Delors was indeed the architect and supporter of these free-market, laissez-faire policies and plans. This was pointed out at the time by Michie (1998) and others, including the late Wynne Godley, the former Director of Cambridge's Department of Applied Economics:

> It is thus an extraordinary fact about Maastricht that the only new institution to be created is a new independent central bank to run monetary policy. How is the rest of economic policy supposed to be run? How in particular is fiscal policy supposed to be determined? The authors of the Treaty appear to think that provided you have a central bank to conduct monetary policy, fiscal policy and every other aspect of economic policy can be resolved by laying down one or two simple rules, for instance that countries should normally balance their budget. Now I think this is a very impoverished and inadequate proposal, and I am forced to the conclusion that it could only have been made by people who think that nothing more is needed. That is, people who follow the new consensus and are prepared to base all their recommendations on the idea that economies are basically self-righting systems. It should be remembered that the Delors Committee, which was the forerunner of Maastricht, was predominantly composed of central bankers; the proposal to place all power in the hands of the central bank should perhaps not be so surprising . . . we have been down this road before. The need for active fiscal and exchange rate policies in the 1920s came up against the orthodoxy of the day, that public spending would crowd out private investment and that currency adjustments could be effected with a fixed exchange rate system by forcing down domestic wages and prices. Those truths were wrong then and they are wrong today. (Godley, 1993, n.p.)

. . .the rich countries did not develop on the basis of the policies and institutions that they now recommend to, and often force upon, the developing countries. . . .

We can only conclude that, whether intentionally or not, the rich countries are effectively 'kicking away the ladder' that allowed them to climb to where they are now. (Chang, 2011, pp. 465 and 472)

3.5 The nature of economics: 'shedding darkness'[7]

This book focuses on globalisation as an economic phenomenon, whilst recognising of course that there are many other aspects – political, social, cultural – and with important literatures around globalisation and democracy (Rudra, 2005). However, as will no doubt be evident from the above discussion, to understand the economics of globalisation requires an appreciation of historical, institutional and evolutionary factors that are generally missing from mainstream economic theory.

The political economy of Smith, Ricardo and Marx was concerned with uncovering the laws of motion of the capitalist system, analysing the distribution of income between the classes, and seeking to determine the implications of this for the future trajectory of the economy and society. As discussed in Chapter 1 above, this 'classical' political economy was in the late 19th century replaced as the economic mainstream by 'neoclassical' economics, which focused on the individual rather than on social classes, and assumed that the economy was driven by utility maximising consumers and profit maximising firms. This new mainstream is also referred to sometimes as 'marginalism', since economic decisions are thought of as being made by these individual

---

7 Joan Robinson (1982) reviewed Axel Leijonhufvud, *Information and Coordination. Essays in Macroeconomic Theory* (OUP, 1981) for the *Cambridge Journal of Economics*; for a flavour of what she thought:

> The analysis purports to deal with a world of growth with 'complete information' apparently about the future as well as the present situation in an economy. 'Certain authors', which include *me*, argue that 'a realistic appreciation of the role of ignorance in the human condition must preclude the use of equilibrium models. However this may be, this paper cannot do without it' (p. 295). But what can it do with it?

My colleague and a founding Editor of the *Cambridge Journal of Economics* Frank Wilkinson recounts that they thanked Joan for her review, but said that they required a title for her piece. She responded that an appropriate title, given what her piece was reviewing, would be 'Shedding Darkness'.

consumers or firms 'at the margin', on whether to consume one more item of X as opposed to Y, and firms deciding whether to produce one more unit of output at the margin, or one less. Particularly for firms, this is not of course how decisions are made.

Chapter 1 concluded by pointing out that one weakness of mainstream economics in general is that policy implications are sometimes assumed, without appreciating that those conclusions were made on the basis of simplifying assumptions. Thus, welfare economics will compare two states of the world where some people are better off in one state, and some better off in the other. Provided that on average one is superior, then that should be chosen, and if this means moving from the current state to that new one, then the winners can compensate the losers, and everyone will be better off. This argument is sometimes used to justify free trade (and globalisation). However, if the winners then fail to compensate the losers, we have a problem. The losers are made worse off, and remain worse off. And when it's proclaimed that the new era is more successful, and people are better off, those who have been made worse off may fail to be impressed. This is, arguably, what has happened with certain aspects of globalisation, and may also have played a part in the vote of the UK electorate to leave the European Union (EU), despite being told that 'the country' and 'the average household' were better off in the EU.[8]

Thus, those campaigning to remain in the EU argued that the resulting inward migration was good for the economy. But the benefits from migration do not impact upon the whole country equally, nor on all individuals equally; and the same goes for the costs. This could have been recognised and dealt with by government, by providing additional funding to help cover the extra costs of social and public services in the areas receiving migrants. Similarly with trade, where the benefits will not be spread evenly within an economy. Crucially, many may be made worse off by losing their jobs, or at least by having their wages depressed even though the jobs remain. Ironically, these negative effects on the parts of the country that tended to vote to leave the EU would have come more from imports from outside the EU than from the EU itself. But it is generally recognised that in contrast with the 'remain' campaign, which had no slogans memorable enough to recall, the 'leave' campaign adopted and repeated

---

8 See for example Colantone and Stanig (2016).

continually their slogan of 'take back control', which was reported as resonating strongly with many voters. Thus, even if the imports that were thought to be replacing local jobs and/or depressing wages and living standards were originating from outside the EU, it may have been thought that membership of the EU was constraining the options available to the UK to deal with the situation. Or just that globalisation was to blame, and if the EU was anything, it was a flagship for globalisation.

The neoclassical assumption that decisions are made by individual actors at the margin – unaffected by what others are doing, thinking and deciding – is critiqued by, for example, Paul Ormerod (2016), who argues that we should be thinking instead in terms of networks, rather than of isolated individuals. Consumers will be influenced by the behaviour of others in their networks: 'Network effects, in fact, can completely swamp the impact of incentives, leading to very different outcomes to the ones intended by those who altered the incentives, whether they are companies or public policymakers'. And networks between firms partly explain the contagion effect of economic crises, where one defaulting firm can trigger further bankruptcies. Ormerod (2016) argues that 'I have heard frequent arguments along the lines: this is all very well, these networks seem very clever, but you lack clear guidelines about what we should actually do to solve a problem. If we use the economically rational approach, we know what to do.' But, Ormerod argues, the 'exact answer to a problem' may lead to policy conclusions that have the exact opposite effect than that intended. As Keynes might have said, better to be roughly right than precisely wrong.[9]

Such network effects are of course important when considering globalisation, and its causes and consequences, as these effects will thereby operate increasingly across borders – and developments in one country may increasingly be the result of what occurs elsewhere globally. On what the implications of all this are for the future of economics as a discipline, my own thoughts are set out in Kitson and Michie (2000) and Foxon et al. (2013), and we return to this in the concluding chapter.

---

9 Apparently incorrectly attributed to Keynes, the original quote 'It is better to be roughly right than precisely wrong' comes from Read (1898, p. 351).

3.6   The importance of place: regions, cities and the locality

The history of capitalism, that is, since the Industrial Revolution, has been one of globalisation – albeit in different forms. It has also been a history of industrial clusters forming across regions, and of urbanisation, as people move to cities for jobs. On the role and importance of regions, and regional resilience in the face of globalisation, see for example Christopherson et al., 2008. On the role of cities, in particular in relation to economic success in the face of competition from other cities nationally and globally, see for example Martin (2016) and Storper et al. (2016). As well as the importance of 'subnational' regions and cities, the importance of local economies should be recognised. A new era of globalisation, pursuing a global Green New Deal, should focus as much on the local as on the global – as well as on the region, the city, and the nation-state. Some argue that globalisation should be replaced by localisation. We would argue that localisation is indeed key, and that as for globalisation, the focus should be on developing a new *form* of globalisation, appropriate for pursuing a Green New Deal globally over the next generation. And an important aspect of that would be to recognise the importance of local economies.

3.7   Contributions from mainstream economics

With the above caveats about mainstream economics in mind, Vernon (1966) nevertheless emphasised usefully the timing of innovation, the effect of scale economies, and the role of uncertainty in influencing shifts in international trade and international investment – as opposed to focusing on comparative costs. Endogenous growth theory was an approach that explicitly dropped any requirement to assume diminishing returns, and on the contrary used R&D as a driver of the long-run rate of growth, and with increased economic integration also feeding through into growth, such that growth became endogenous, in the sense of becoming self-reinforcing through these feedback processes.[10] (That this was seen as going beyond the previous neoclassical growth theory was demonstrated when the young Ed Balls left the *Financial Times* (where he had been a leader writer) in 1994 to work as Gordon Brown's economic adviser, and drafted a speech in which Gordon Brown referred to 'post neo-classical endogenous growth theory',

---

10 See for example Krugman (1979), and Rivera-Batiz and Romer (1991).

much to the amusement of TV comedy panel shows, and even Michael Heseltine, then deputy prime minister, who said in Parliament, 'It's not Brown's. It's Balls.')

In 1992 Henderson et al. proposed a 'global production network' framework for the analysis of economic integration and its relation to the asymmetries of economic and social development. Krugman and Venables (1995) analyse the way in which globalisation can undermine manufacturing in the 'peripheral' countries, contributing towards the inequality of nations. Similarly, Narula and Dunning (2000) analyse the differences between the performance of developing countries (some catching up, some falling behind), including in relation to their bargaining power vis-à-vis the MNCs. Calvo and Mendoza (2000) demonstrate how globalisation promotes contagion. Kaplinsky (2000) reports the way in which participation in the global economy in itself may not provide a path to sustainable income growth or to an equitable distribution of returns, and stresses the importance of the 'value chain' – that is, the range of activities which are required to bring a product or service from conception, through the intermediary phases of production, to delivery to consumers.

Dreher (2006) developed a new index for globalisation made up of economic, social and political integration, arguing that his empirical analysis found that globalisation promoted growth. Note, though, that within a year of publication, globalisation had led to the 2007–2008 global financial crisis and subsequent global recession of 2009. In general, trade is thought to promote growth; see for example Frankel and Romer (1999), although they find the positive effect of trade on income to be only moderately significant. However, as Kitson and Michie (1995) point out, that trade and growth are correlated is not in doubt; however, it is a two-way relation, with growth tending to provoke trade, regardless of the effects of trade on growth. Before turning in Chapter 6 to the practice of globalisation, we first consider the role of technology, and of multinational corporations, in Chapters 4 and 5 respectively.

4 Technology, innovation and globalisation

> What is called globalization is changing the notion of the nation state as power becomes more diffuse and borders more porous. Technological change is reducing the power and capacity of government to control its domestic economy free from external influence.
> (Tony Blair, speaking to executives of Rupert Murdoch's News Corporation, quoted in the *Financial Times*, 20 March 1996)

The most obvious way in which today's globalisation is qualitatively different from just a few years ago is the ubiquitous availability and use of communication technologies and social media that enable people to communicate globally, transferring data and images almost instantaneously. One widely quoted example was the way in which anti-government protestors in Egypt in 2011 were able to organise large protests in Tahrir Square in Cairo at such short notice, done almost entirely through mobile phones and social media. And it wasn't just co-ordinating and mobilising people – the activities of the protesters and the actions of the army could be filmed and broadcast live across the globe, from mobile phones.

Other globalising innovations include blockchain, which serves as the public ledger for bitcoin transactions, and with other possible uses including global online course accreditation. Learning in general is becoming increasingly web-based, quite apart from the growth of online courses and degrees, and MOOCs – the Massive, Open, Online Courses. Driverless cars are emerging, and high-speed rail expanding. The need for green technologies is spurring a range of new technologies, which are global both in the challenge they are being developed to deal with, and in their use and application. Likewise health technologies, from stem-cell applications through to the challenge of dealing with global pandemics.

As discussed in Chapter 1, all this is new, in the sense that we haven't been here before. But in the pre-First World War era of globalisation there would have been similar talk of new global communication technologies, from telegrams to telephones; and new and improved transportation technologies from rail to the motorcar and the aeroplane. Looking out the window of our train journey through time we would in both instances agree that everything today is totally different than previously – save that we would be saying the same thing in both eras – that everything is totally different. One common feature over the past century and a half of globalisation, through its different eras, is that technology and innovation have been both facilitators and drivers of globalisation.

4.1   Technology and innovation as facilitators of globalisation

In so far as globalisation involves the movement of people and goods across the world, transport clearly plays a crucial facilitating role. The vast migrations during the first era of post-Industrial Revolution globalisation, across Europe, from Europe to America, and across America were all made possible by developments in rail and shipping transport, and the ability of companies to operate across these distances was facilitated by the new developments in communication technologies.

Today, air transport plays a huge role, and innovations continue, including drones which are fighting US wars (declared or not) globally, as well as promising us all home deliveries of consumer products. Ever larger container ships carry goods across the world, and new technologies enable these vessels to be piloted with fewer – if any – staff. This global transport industry, particularly the flying of people and goods across the world, is a major source of the carbon emissions that cause climate change, and hence their growing use may prove unsustainable. Certainly in terms of goods, this may lead to pressure to row back on globalisation, with a greater emphasis on sourcing locally, rather than shipping or flying across the world components and goods which could be produced just as well and easily without the degree of environmental damage that is currently being wreaked by air-flight and other modes of transportation.

4.2   Technology and innovation as drivers of globalisation

As described in Chapter 2, one of the drivers of globalisation has for a long time been firms seeking to expand their activities across borders in order to find new areas for profitable sales and production, as well as to source raw material and other inputs. New technological developments can drive this in two ways. If the domestic firm develops the technology, it will give it an added incentive to produce overseas (as well as at home), since it will be well placed to sell its products in those new markets, exploiting its technological advantage. Conversely, if the new technologies are developed overseas, this may create an incentive to operate in that area, to benefit from that new technology – either directly, by for example buying up the foreign firm with the new technology, or indirectly if they are able to some extent to mimic the new technology, and are able to hire workers and suppliers familiar with that technology.[1] This sharing of expertise and skills, which may be through quite informal networking, is often an important factor in the economic success of industrial districts, regions and networks. These are, thus, important areas for industrial, regional and innovation policy to work on and invest in. Even more so if climate change is to be tackled by increasing local and regional economic activities in place of today's transporting of goods and components across the globe, to no great effect.

The important role of industrial districts was first drawn attention to and analysed by Alfred Marshall in his *Principles of Economics* (1890). Considered to be one of the founders of modern economics, Marshall referred to a 'thickly peopled industrial district' when firms cluster geographically, providing what today would be referred to as positive agglomeration effects. Such industrial districts, or networks, have developed in different forms across the globe – with Silicon Valley perhaps the best known. Today, small and medium sized enterprises in such areas would tend to have strong links both with other firms in the district – including their competitors – and at the same time other firms globally, made easier than ever with developments in communication and computing technologies.

---

1   Florida (1997) examines the globalisation of innovation and the phenomenon of foreign direct investment in research and development, and concludes that the globalisation of innovation is driven in large measure by technology factors, with the objective of firms to secure access to scientific and technical human capital being of particular importance.

The importance of regional resilience in economic activity is analysed in detail by Christopherson et al. (2008), who stress the importance of the 'region' – meaning the sub-national region, rather that the 'regional blocks' of nations such as the European Union – in economic activity.[2] They argue that the importance of regions – and of regional resilience – should be not just noted or welcomed, but should be actively worked upon, to ensure that all the possible benefits are fully developed.[3] For a different analysis which also stresses the importance of regions – and cities – within the process of economic growth and globalisation, see Scott and Storper (2003).

4.3 The theory and practice of technology, innovation and globalisation

Knowledge and technology clearly play a vital role in the competitiveness of firms in international markets, and hence in the success of the economies in which those firms are based and from which they operate. Yet until relatively recently, economics as a discipline did not devote much attention to studying the ways in which knowledge actually leads to the generation and diffusion of technological innovation. From the 1980s onwards, more attention was paid, although often by those on the fringes of mainstream economics (see in particular Rosenberg, 1982 and 1994; Dosi, 1988; and Freeman, 1994). The crucial lesson learned from such research is that the process that nurtures and disseminates technological change involves a complex web of interactions among a range of different subjects and institutions (David and Foray, 1995). As argued by Archibugi and Michie (1997b, p. 2) in the introduction to a book which analyses these issues in detail (and from which the above paragraph draws):

> These various aspects of the process are unlikely to be 'captured' in their entirety by looking at standard economic variables such as prices and quantities alone. To understand technological change it is crucial to identify the economic, social, political and geographical context in which innovation is generated and disseminated. This space may be local, national or global. Or, more likely, it will involve a complex and evolving integration, at different levels, of local, national and global factors.

---

2 See Christopherson et al., 2010, pp. 3–10.
3 On measuring regions' capacity for resilience, as well as actual outcomes in terms of resilience, see Sensier et al., 2016.

On the role played by national and global forces in shaping technological advance, Archibugi and Michie (1997b, p. 2) argue:

> Certainly, a globalized economy is transforming the landscape for the generation and diffusion of innovation, but this does not appear to decrease the importance of national characteristics nor, even less, of national institutions and their policies. On the contrary, by magnifying the potential costs and benefits which will result from any one country's competitive advantage or disadvantage – as a growing proportion of the home market risks being lost to imports, while a growing proportion of domestic output may be dependent on winning export orders – globalization will increase the impact which national policy will have on domestic living standards.

McMillan and Rodrik (2014, p. 28) draw a similar conclusion:

> Structural change, like economic growth itself, is not an automatic process. It needs a nudge in the appropriate direction, especially when a country has a strong comparative advantage in natural resources. Globalization does not alter this underlying reality. But it does increase the costs of getting the policies wrong, just as it increases the benefits of getting them right.

Patel and Pavitt (1991) found that the technology activities of large firms tend to be located disproportionately in the firms' home countries – hence their paper's sub-title being 'an important case of "non-globalisation"'. Patel (1995) found that despite the increasing globalisation of markets and production during the 1980s, there was no systematic evidence of any globalisation of technology. Again, he found evidence that technology production tends to stay close to the home base, even in face of globalisation. Patel and Vega (1999) found that firms tend to locate their technology abroad in their core areas where they are strong at home. This suggests that adapting products and processes and materials to suit foreign markets, and providing technical support to off-shore manufacturing plants, remain major factors underlying the internationalisation of technology. It is also consistent with the notion that firms are increasingly engaging in small scale activities to monitor and scan new technological developments in centres of excellence in foreign countries within their areas of existing strength. Storper (1992) found that the increasing export specialisation cannot be explained by the Ricardian 'comparative advantage' of standard trade theory; instead, he concludes that the empirically visible patterns must be due to technological or absolute advantage, and this in turn leads to the creation of 'technology districts'. Consistent with all three of these studies, Archibugi and Michie (1995) researched three aspects of the globalisation of technology, namely the global *exploitation* of technology, global technological *collaboration*, and the global *generation* of technology, with the results obtained for each of the three categories suggesting that the role of national innovation policy is not necessarily becoming less important because of globalisation, concluding that:

> The exploitation of innovations requires national governments to settle the regime according to which new technologies can be exploited within their borders. International collaborations rely on the nature of the national technological capabilities associated with the prospective partner. As for the generation of innovation, this is still largely organized within the boundaries of nation-states. These results – suggesting that the role of nations in the organization of innovative activities remains crucial – are consistent with the new body of literature emphasizing the role of national systems in organizing and promoting innovation (see Porter, 1990; Lundvall, 1992; Nelson, 1993). More importantly, the categorization proposed suggests that the dichotomy global/national is a false one. (Archibugi and Michie, 1995, p. 134)

Cantwell (1995) on the other hand rejects the hypothesis that innovations are almost always located in the home countries of the parent company, and finds that the international dispersion of activity tends to be led by the technology leaders, who may then innovate overseas. Kuemmerle (1999), however, finds that whilst firms do indeed invest in R&D sites abroad, the R&D tends to occur at home in the first instance, prior to then being transmitted abroad.

4.4   Systems of innovation

The different results reported above (in particular Cantwell and Pavitt) are consistent with the processes described previously in this chapter. A domestic company may innovate, or a multinational may innovate in its home country, and this will provide an added impetus to expand overseas to exploit this technological advantage. At the same time a separate and additional impetus to expand overseas may be to benefit from technological leadership in other countries. But to benefit from such technologies, companies must have sufficient 'absorptive capacity' to be able to understand, adopt, and utilise technologies from outside their organisation, and this in turn may require a degree of R&D to be conducted internally – preferably in the country from which it is hoped that 'outside' technologies will be absorbed. And if the multinational is therefore conducting R&D overseas in order to create and maintain sufficient absorptive capacity to be able to benefit fully from the advanced technologies over there, then it is likely that the multinational will therefore itself innovate in that country, as a result of the R&D that it is undertaking. So the linkages and causal processes are complex, but certainly it would be expected that there will be a number of drivers, some tending to lead multinationals to research and innovate at home, and others tending to lead to them researching and innovating in host countries.[4] In both cases, it is clear that knowledge and technological innovation play a crucial role in economic activities. Archibugi and Michie (1997b) argue that:

> While this has long been recognized by managers, scientists and engineers, it is only really over the past decade or so that economists have devoted much effort to studying the way in which knowledge actually leads to the generation and diffusion of technological innovation. This attention has, however, produced a vast literature which has begun to shine some light into the 'black box' of the relationship between technology and the productive process (see, in particular, Rosenberg, 1982, 1994). The initial hypotheses in a handful of pioneering works during the 1950s and 1960s on the economic determinants and impact of innovation have since been corroborated by a substantial amount of theoretical and empirical research.

Howells and Michie (1998) analyse three elements of the 'globalisation of technology': the *geographical* extent in terms of the spatial spread and intensity (or 'depth'); *sectoral* variations; and the *'temporal'* extent – that is, when effectively did the phenomenon emerge and develop? With this framework, they find first a far from uniform 'globalisation', and second that government policy at the national level is crucially important, in part because much of what is depicted as globalisation is very clearly inter-national.

Iammarino and Michie (1998, pp. 350–351) present empirical evidence on each of a number of processes identified through which technology and innovation are becoming increasingly globalised, finding that:

> The picture in each case is rather complex and does not appear consistent with a view that the role of individual nations and governments are being swept aside by a technologically driven global economy. Certainly the world

---

4 For a number of key contributions on the issues of systems of innovation as related to globalisation, see Archibugi and Michie (1997b).

economy is becoming increasingly international, and the operation of many corporations is becoming more global. But much of this is a continuation of trends witnessed before, some of which have even been reversed during certain historical periods. And some of the processes that are often depicted as 'global' would be more accurately depicted as 'regional'. Much of the action is taking place within and between the tripolar grouping of developed countries, of the EU, NAFTA and the Pacific Rim countries. Finally, the data suggest that some countries are winning out in the increased global competition over innovation and the exploitation of technological advance. Insofar as these results are either analogous to, or at least contribute towards, the broader processes of economic globalization, the message is that globalization is not replacing the fact of – or need for – corporate and governmental strategies and policy action. Rather, it is that these corporate and national strategies are increasingly being played out within an arena that is global.

Thus, the data do indeed indicate certain trends towards technological globalization, and these changes involve 'winners and losers'. Within the literature on technological globalization and National Systems of Innovation, Cantwell (1995) argues that national patterns of specialization tend to be reinforced, rather than destroyed, by the international integration of activities of MNEs. This conclusion finds further support from the new evidence reported in this paper. Accordingly, globalization and national systems of innovation should be seen as complements, rather than as opposing concepts.

Archibugi et al. (1999b) argue that a proper understanding of technological developments and their dissemination throughout the economy and society requires us to understand the social fabric that shapes these developments, and that the notion of systems of innovation – local, regional, sectoral and national – helps to explain the interactions between agents that generate and use technology. New technologies have always been international in scope: the transmission of knowledge has never respected states' borders; thus:

There is a complex interplay between technological change and globalization. On the one hand, new technologies act as a powerful vehicle for the diffusion of information across distant communities. For example, it would be difficult to imagine the current globalization of financial markets without the existence of the new information and communication technologies, since they have made it possible to obtain instant transactions across the world. On the other hand, the process of generating and diffusing new technologies has been molded and strengthened by the flows of individuals, commodities and capital. This has created a circular process whereby technology has facilitated globalization and vice versa. (Archibugi et al. 1999b, p. 534)

Howells (2011, p. 113) argues that the systems of innovation approach is both robust and flexible in its ability to absorb conceptual developments and empirical findings from the wider literatures on innovation, multinational and organisational studies.

4.5   The R&D activities of multinationals

The way that multinational corporations approach their research and development is analysed in detail by the various contributors to Archibugi and Michie (1997b). In 'The myth of economic globalization', Kleinknecht and ter Wengel (1998) argue that international trade and investment is more a case of the world's major trading blocs becoming more integrated with each other, with the share of foreign direct investment FDI taken by low-wage countries showing little growth. They ascribe this in part to the reasons that Marshall gave originally for 'industrial districts', with companies benefiting from pools of skilled workers, specialised suppliers, and technological spillovers, including via tacit knowledge – factors which may prove more important than relative prices or wage levels.[5]

4.6   Conclusion

As argued by Stiglitz (2016b), there is widespread discontent across the world at the current mixture of economic stagnation and inequality:

> Globalisation is, of course, only one part of what is going on; technological innovation is another part. But all of this openness and disruption were *supposed* to make us richer, and the advanced countries could have introduced policies to ensure that the gains were widely shared.

> Instead, they pushed for policies that restructured markets in ways that increased inequality and undermined economic performance; growth actually slowed as the rules of the game were rewritten to advance the interests of banks and corporations – the rich and powerful – at the expense of

---

5 For a detailed discussion of trade and innovation, see the various contributions to Archibugi and Michie (1998).

everyone else. Workers' bargaining power was weakened; in the US, at least, competition laws didn't keep up with the times; and existing laws were inadequately enforced. Financialization continued apace and corporate governance worsened. . . .

The main message of *Globalization and its Discontents* was that the problem was not globalization, but how the process was being managed. Unfortunately, the management didn't change. Fifteen years later, the new discontents have brought that message home to the advanced economies.

Thus, technological change and innovation play an important role in economic developments, including as regards globalisation. But innovation is just one factor, and has to be seen in the context of other drivers – economic, social, and political. Indeed, the current form of free-market globalisation will have itself shaped – or distorted – the nature of innovation, with far greater resources going into the development of 'new financial produces' (collatoralising debt, and so forth) than would otherwise have been the case. Further, regarding the quote from Tony Blair at the start of this chapter, technology cannot be properly blamed for an inability of governments to act. It is true that technology can be used to, for example, try to evade laws, but equally, technology can be used to enforce laws. Public policy remains key.

5 Multinationals, corporate diversity and globalisation

> We enable our clients' success by constantly seeking suitable solutions to their problems. We will do what is right – not just what is allowed.
>
> (Deutsche Bank, *Code of Ethics*, 2013)[1]

Perraton (2011, pp. 71–72) reports that:

> Foreign direct investment by multinational corporations has grown faster than trade, let alone income, over the post-war period and sales by foreign affiliates of MNCs are now more than double global exports. MNCs account for a significant minority of private GDP, particularly in manufacturing, and, on some estimates, a majority of world trade (with a quarter or more of world trade being between branches of the same company). As major international borrowers and savers, MNCs have been central to the development of global finance. Although FDI remains a minority of total investment, it is growing and significant.

5.1 The growth of multinationals

What might be termed the current literature on multinational corporations (as opposed to classical works such as Hilferding's *Finance Capital*) began perhaps with John Dunning's 1973 seminal piece on 'The determinants of international production' in which he both explored the origins and growth of the multinational enterprise as an organisational form, and placed this theoretically within the context of an analysis of both international trade in goods, and international trade in factors of production. This represented a major contribution to industrial organisation theory.[2]

---

1 Cited in Caesar (2016).

2 For further analysis of how multinational corporations have affected globalisation and vice versa, see for example Cantwell and Narula (2001), Melitz (2003) and Buckley and Ghauri (2004).

The growth in the activities of multinationals has led governments to compete to attract inward investment from them. The hope of course is that the foreign owned firms will be more efficient and dynamic than their domestic counterparts because they can exploit cost differences across countries and utilise intangible assets more fully, in which case the inward investment should have a positive impact on both productivity and employment. However, foreign ownership may reflect monopolisation of an industry, or restructuring associated with international mergers and acquisitions, in which case it is unlikely that such foreign ownership will be associated with higher employment, and the effects on productivity growth may prove to be either positive or negative. Thus:

> Theoretical explanations for FDI predict that the relationship between FDI and employment growth could be positive or negative. Similarly there is no clear cut theoretical prediction concerning the effects of multinational activity on productivity growth, although Hymer's theory of monopolistic advantage and the transactions costs approach both suggest that high technology firms with intangible assets are more likely to become multinational. Despite the ambiguities of the theoretical evidence there appears to be a widespread perception amongst policy makers that inward FDI raises employment and productivity growth. Accordingly, a large number of countries have introduced policies to attract multinationals through both deregulation and financial and other inducements.

> The evidence presented in this paper suggests that such a policy approach is not well grounded in the evidence on the relationship between multinational activity and employment and productivity growth. Using cross section data for the US and Europe's four largest economies we find no evidence of a positive impact of multinationals activity on employment growth. (Michie, Oughton and Ramirez, 2002, pp. 180-181)

The actual outcome of such investment will depend on the extent to which productive co-operation is forged with other firms and institutions domestically and internationally. This will in turn depend upon – or at least be influenced by – public policy:

> To get the most from footloose capital and transnational economic organisation, national governments need to focus on how to upgrade their own domestic economies. Firstly, this will maximise the chance of domestic firms being able to forge international links and benefit from them. Secondly the domestic economy will thereby prove attractive to the sort of inward

investment that is likely to contribute rather than just take advantage of the domestic economy. And thirdly, it will maximise the beneficial impact that such investment is likely to have in terms of linking with domestic firms and contributing positively to the existing national systems of innovation. (Michie, Oughton and Zanfei, 2002, pp. 9–10)

5.2   Multinational corporations (MNCs) and globalisation

Ietto-Gillies (2011) argues that one of the major differences between the current era of globalisation and previous eras is in the role played by MNCs, which participate in a range of transactions and flows between countries, including trade in goods and services; foreign direct investment; profits, interest and dividends repatriated from the various types of overseas investment; inter-organisational collaborative partnerships; and movement of people across borders. In terms of policy implications, Ietto-Gillies (2011) sets these out for two areas of economic activity: the financial sector, and MNCs.[3] On the financial sector, Ietto-Gillies (2011, pp. 178–179) argues that:

1. There has been excessive, unsustainable growth of the financial sector over the last 30 years.
2. This growth is connected with the liberal, market ideology in politics, business and much of the economics profession.
3. This growth together with a variety of government regulations ranging from taxation to the liberalisation of the labour market have had a huge impact on the changes in the distribution of income and wealth in favour of the rich. (Atkinson and Piketty, 2007; Lankester, 2009).
4. The growth of the financial sector has had a negative impact on the real sector of economies; it has also made the economic system as a whole more unstable.
5. The unregulated flows of finance across countries have made the world more interconnected and this has made the crisis more devastating for smaller and fragile economies such as Iceland, Ireland, Greece, the Eastern European and the developing countries. (Wade, 2009).

She goes on to argue that increased regulation is required, and that this should take account of both institutional and systemic risk, and should include the following:

---

3 Note that Ietto-Gillies (2011) refers to transnational corporations; in the cited passages this has been changed to the term used in the current book, namely multinational corporations.

1. Separation of financial institutions according to the type and level of institutional risk involved. Specifically: institutions dealing with commercial banking; with long-term borrowing and lending (that is, housing mortgages); and with investment banking. Such separation would diminish future risks for the institutions as well as the system as a whole. It would also lead to a smaller size for financial institutions, thus avoiding future situations in which an institution is deemed too big to fail; moreover, it would inject more competition into the system with benefits for consumers.

2. The financial sector and those strata of society that benefited most from deregulation should now be bearing the cost of the global financial crisis, for which they were responsible.

3. There should be strong regulatory authorities and frameworks at the national level.

4. At the international level, the crisis has highlighted the need for a new, regulatory institutional architecture dealing with cross-border flows, with tax revenue issues, and with rescue packages.

5. A tax on cross-border financial transactions is long overdue.

These points are discussed in subsequent chapters, in particular regarding taxation, and the global 'architecture'. On multinational corporations, Ietto-Gillies (2011, p. 181) argues that national governments need to develop policies to deal with the powerful position that MNCs now have:

> We need regulation to channel the many opportunities and cope with the many problems raised by the new technologies and by the MNCs' activities (in relation to the environment, safety, competition and labour standards). Many problems cannot be tackled without appropriate international institutions. Self-regulation is unlikely to work for most issues, including those related to the environmental and to labour standards; in the end these standards will always be in the way of profit-making. Moreover, self-regulation cannot secure the coordination within and between industries necessary for the long-term prosperity of companies and countries.

We need more coordination power within and across frontiers, by other actors. There is therefore a need to implement policies designed to develop countervailing transnational power in the other actors, be they labour, multinational companies, consumers or governments themselves. This will enable these actors to participate fully and actively in the globalisation process and will make the process more inclusive.

In a world in which much activity takes place across borders, there is an increased need for transnational governance as well as for the strengthening of national and regional governance. This can be achieved *via* the establishment of appropriate supranational institutions among whose aims should be the monitoring of transnational business activities.

This last point, on the need for global monitoring of MNCs, is one that has been stressed in a number of publications over the years by Roger Sugden, amongst others.

5.3   The control of MNCs

Epstein (2011) discusses the debates over whether MNCs have positive or negative impacts on the host and home countries, and over the relative impacts on rich and poor countries, and upon labour and environmental standards, concluding that:

> Despite the fact that there has been a great deal of research during the last several decades on MNCs, there is no consensus on their effects. Still, the evidence that does exist suggests the following: though foreign direct investment can have positive impacts on home and host countries, the likelihood that these positive effects will materialise and be widely shared is greatly diminished by the 'neo-liberal' policy framework that is dominant in much of the world today. I conclude that what is needed, instead of more deregulation and 'free' capital mobility, is a more democratic framework of multinational investment regulation to help countries and their citizens reap the benefits that can be associated with international investment. If this was done properly, the tensions that arise between the interests of southern and northern workers might be significantly reduced. (Epstein, 2011, pp. 185–186)

After a detailed analysis of the theoretical and empirical evidence regarding the impact of MNCs on employment, wages, technological spill-over effects and other potential impacts on the host countries in particular, Epstein concludes that at best the evidence is mixed, and that:

> There is no evidence that the push by international organisations such as the IMF, World Bank, OECD and WTO to promote more FDI liberalisation is well-founded theoretically or empirically. These organisations should desist in this promotion, unless and until there is stronger evidence that

such investment is beneficial within the current regulatory environment. The implication of this moratorium on investment liberalisation would be a much greater tolerance by the international financial institutions of a variety of national regulatory regimes toward foreign investment, regimes that suit the particular circumstances of different countries. Finally, continued efforts by governments and international institutions should be undertaken to develop mechanisms to reduce 'prisoner's dilemma' outcomes, which are so likely in this current environment. Among the measures that should be considered are floors on taxation, subsidies and environmental regulations, and the increased commitment to the enforcement of core labour standards.[4] (Epstein, 2011, p. 197)

Braunstein (2011) points out that another disputed area regarding the impact of MNCs and foreign direct investment – alongside the disputes around their impact on employment, wages and innovation, and on labour and employment standards – concerns the differential impact on men and women. After a detailed analysis of the evidence on the range of such impacts, she concludes that:

While there has been a positive relationship between women's employment and FDI in semi-industrialised countries, there is mounting evidence that women either lose these jobs to more qualified men as industries upgrade or get pushed down the production chain into subcontracted work, as competition forces firms to continually lower costs. There is likely to be some short-term improvement in women's incomes as FDI expands, but the longer-term trajectory of women's wages is less promising. These findings are consistent with those that indicate that trade and FDI have done little to narrow the gender wage gap. In terms of how to manage FDI for the good of gender equality and development, the main obstacles are the constraints posed by international competition in export markets and the neoliberal orientation of the global policy environment. Addressing these issues requires both international coordination and national industrial policies. (Braunstein, 2011, p. 209)

Many developing countries seek to attract inward investment in order to provide relatively skilled jobs, thereby enhancing their 'human capital'. However, research suggests that this is essentially the wrong way round: any such inward investment may or may not have that desired effect, whereas one of the surest ways of attracting inward

---

4 Epstein cites Heintz (2011) and Braunstein and Epstein (1999) for further discussion of these issues.

investment – particularly of the sort being sought in this context – is precisely to invest in public education and training, in effect enhancing the country's human capital which will, amongst other things, act as an attractor to investment – from overseas and domestically. Thus:

> If human capital enhancement is one of the outcomes hoped for from inward investment, then public policy can usefully operate along two routes simultaneously. First, by education and training, enhancing human capital directly as a means, amongst other things, of attracting inward investment. Such a policy, which has been followed explicitly by a number of governments, can be expected to have a positive impact on both the quantity and the quality (type, or nature) of inward investment.
>
> Second, though, there are a range of policy measures that can be taken to get the most out of the inward investment once it has arrived, both in terms of further advancing human capital and more generally. The question is how to encourage MNEs to invest in human capital enhancement. The key mechanisms, it is suggested, are those already being pursued, not all of which are obviously connected with human capital. Thus public education is vital. But so are policies to enhance technological diffusion. Firstly such policies will inevitably lead to further intervention from government and other public agencies to enhance human capital as requirements and opportunities become uncovered. Secondly, technological diffusion will increase the incentives for companies to take advantage of these technologies, which will in turn require human capital enhancement. And thirdly it will be an attractor not only to further FDI, but to FDI going into relatively high value added areas. (Michie, 2002, p. 370)

5.4   Public ownership

The 1945–1975 Golden Age of Capitalism saw a deliberate effort at planned or co-ordinated globalisation, following the disarray of the years following the First World War, which witnessed the speculative boom of the 'roaring 20s' culminating in the 1929 Wall Street Crash and subsequent Great Depression with mass unemployment globally, along with fascist regimes in Germany, Italy, Spain and Portugal and a militarist regime in Japan. In Europe particularly, 'no return to the 30s' was a strong political rallying call and demand during and immediately following the Second World War. Government commitments to restore and maintain full employment, through sustained economic growth, was in most European countries to be delivered through a combination – which varied from country to country – of public ownership, planning, fiscal and monetary policy, industrial policy, regional policy, and trade union recognition and involvement – but in all cases including a degree of public ownership. This generally included public ownership of the basic utilities of water, gas and electricity; the communications network of post and telecoms; the transport networks of road and rail, and often also airlines, bus companies, ports and shipping; and often other industries such as coal, steel and shipbuilding.

Much of that was lost with the privatisations of the 1980s onwards, which handed these sectors to, or sometimes back to, the private sector (which in general had previously done a poor job, hence leading to nationalisation in the first place). The resulting era of capitalism unleashed (1985–2008), marked by privatisation, deregulation, demutualisation, financialisation, a weakening of trade unions, and cuts in top-rate taxes certainly suffered from greater instability, uncertainty and inequality than the previous Golden Age of Capitalism (1945–1975). On the other hand, the latter era saw a greater fall in world poverty, largely as a result of the huge numbers lifted out of poverty through the rapid development of the Chinese economy. Successive Chinese governments have made great use of free-market policies, including privatisation and deregulation. But caution is required in attributing these successes – of lifting people out of poverty – to laissez-faire capitalism, privatisation and deregulation, as much of the Chinese economy remains state owned, and almost all of it (including the private sector), remains tightly regulated.

Thus, in September 2016 the UK confirmed plans to build a major new nuclear power station (at Hinkley Point C). In the past, this would have been undertaken by the UK's public sector. However, there is little capability or capacity left in the UK's public sector, as a result of privatisation. It should be noted that one of the arguments in favour of privatisation and against nationalisation is that the private sector is more efficient. So, presumably this more efficient UK private sector, to whom the assets, expertise, capacity and capabilities were transferred, would undertake the task? No. Why not? Good question; but one which has not been even asked by the UK government, let alone answered. Instead, this is to be delivered by the French and Chinese. A good example of globalisation. But is that the French and Chinese private sectors? No, it's the French and Chinese public sectors. So, an example of public sector globalisation – stepping in where the UK private sector was inadequate, and the UK public sector had been deliberately weakened. The UK's nuclear sector will therefore have gone from the (successful) public sector to the (inadequate) private sector and back to the public sector – but this time to the French and Chinese public sectors.

And it's not just in providing the productive and social infrastructure that the public sector generally does a better job than the private sector. Mazzucato (2013) has detailed the way in which innovation, entrepreneurship and technological progress all depend crucially on the public sector. One example she gives is what many might take to be the iconic representation of the highest stage of consumer capitalism – the iPhone, the success of which accounts in large measure for the enormous increase in wealth (and associated power) accumulated by Apple since the launch of the iPhone. Yet every aspect of the iPhone, including all the elements that make the smartphone 'smart', was the product of public sector investment and development.

5.5   Corporate diversity

The Ownership Commission was established in the UK in 2010 to consider the different forms of corporate ownership – shareholder-owned, government-owned, family-owned, member-owned, and so on – and to advise on the advantages and disadvantages of each, and the appropriate mix.[5] Its 2012 report argues that each form does indeed have particular advantages or at least possibilities, and that for a resilient economy, it is best to have a healthy mixture of the different corporate forms:

> Plurality of forms of ownership provides more opportunity to align the form of ownership with the appropriate business model, promotes more resilience to shocks within particular sectors and the wider economy, allows investors and savers more avenues in which to save and invest and gives consumers more choice. (Ownership Commission, 2012, p. 10)

The Commission's members undertook case-study visits to the US and Singapore, and looked at other evidence globally. The key point about the benefits of corporate diversity was seen from across the globe, and

---

5 By way of disclosure: I was a member of the Commission, and the research work for the Commission was undertaken by the Oxford Centre for Mutual & Employee-owned Business, of which I am Director.

is something that should be actively promoted. The UK's 2010–2015 Coalition government did commit themselves to bringing this about, including in the financial services sector, and in particular by promoting mutuals – or member-owned firms – to this end. However, they proposed no measure of corporate diversity by which their success in achieving these goals might be met. Michie and Oughton therefore designed such a measure – of corporate diversity – and found that for the financial services sector this aim was not achieved: if anything, the situation actually deteriorated, with the sector becoming even less corporately diverse over time (Michie and Oughton, 2013, 2014).

The degree of corporate diversity in the Asia Pacific Region, and in particular the role of co-operatives and mutuals (that is, member-owned companies) in contributing to this, is analysed and reported in Michie and Rowley (2014) and Rowley and Michie (2014). Here it seems that there may be more promise, although how the Chinese economy develops will clearly have an important bearing.[6]

5.6   Corporate Social Responsibility

It might be asked whether some of the problems caused by privately-owned and shareholder-owned firms might not be solved through the route of Corporate Social Responsibility (CSR). Jenkins (2005) for example does discuss the degree to which Corporate Social Responsibility programmes might alleviate poverty in the context of globalisation. Bakan argues:

> There are good reasons to be sceptical, however, especially when . . . new approaches to CSR demand only that corporations *share* value with social and environmental concerns, but not *sacrifice* it to those concerns. As such, while the new CSR undoubtedly inspires broader social and environmental initiatives from MNCs, its demand that corporations pursue social and environmental good only when it helps them do well – that CSR initiatives necessarily 'intersect with [an MNC's] particular business', as Porter and Kramer describe it – profoundly narrows possibilities. . . .

> CSR, even in its newly broadened ideations, remains limited and problematic: one step forward, perhaps, for its providing some protection of social

---

6 Mayer (2013) argues persuasively that we also need to change the nature of the current shareholder-owned corporate model, to engender a greater degree of trust in their operations.

and environmental values, but three steps back for molding regulatory debates to prioritize business interests, helping justify governments' retreat from mandatory norms, and promoting narratives of corporate change to pacify potential critics. It would, of course, be different if there were broad convergence among business, social, and environmental interests. In reality, however, the social and environmental initiatives that plausibly converge with business interests constitute a 'very narrow subset that involve little cost, little risk, and little disruption to business as usual', as Charles Eisenstein describes it. That is the conclusion not only of commentators, but also many CEOs who report feeling caught in cycles of 'individual, small-scale projects, programs and business units with an incremental impact on sustainability metrics', while 'their responsibilities to more traditional fundamentals of business success, and to the expectation of markets and stakeholders, are preventing greater scale, speed and impact'. Sustainability cannot be achieved, these CEOs believe, 'without radical, structural change to markets and systems'.

The limits of 'shared value' CSR, and, by implication, private regulation, are profound, which is likely the reason 'no significant move has been made [through private regulation] . . . to tame multinational corporate misconduct in respect of [major global issues]'. When social and environmental interests depend for their protection on measures that must cohere with business interests, the 'severe hardship, injustice, imbalance and crisis linked to the rise of private global rulers' are likely to go largely unchecked. Bakan (2015, pp. 294, 297–298, emphasis in the original)

5.7 Conclusion

The Transatlantic Trade and Investment Partnership (TTIP) has been interpreted as a proposed trade agreement that would hand even more powers from elected governments to large corporations. War on Want have warned that the TTIP would 'open the door' to products currently banned in the EU 'for public health and environmental reasons'. According to Greenpeace, 'the EU position is bad, and the US position is terrible'.[7] Young (2016) argues that opposition within both North America and Europe comes 'not primarily from firms and workers fearing increased economic competition, but from less traditional trade actors – consumer and environmental groups and citizens –

---

7 See Owen Jones, Protest never changes anything? Look at how this trade deal has been derailed, *The Guardian*, 5 May 2016.

concerned about the erosion of valued regulations' (p. 345). The EU's consultation on granting new legal rights to companies received 150,000 responses, 97 per cent of which were hostile. By September 2016 such opposition was being expressed also by government ministers in Germany, France, Belgium and Austria. However, even if the TTIP is defeated, the Comprehensive Economic and Trade Agreement between the EU and Canada is just as bad. It gives companies the right to sue governments when they believe their 'future anticipated profits' might be threatened by new laws that those governments might wish to introduce. There is also a 'Trade in Services Agreement' being negotiated by the EU with the US and 21 other countries, which has a similarly anti-democratic approach.[8]

Bakan argues that governments have been removing laws that were introduced to restrict what had been deemed to be unacceptable behaviours of banks and other corporations. He argues that this process could and should be reversed:

> . . . when corporations adversely affect social and environmental interests, it is *because* they are enabled, incentivized, and licensed to do so by mandatory state law. By corollary, law can disable, dis-incentivize, and limit that license, which is why, despite the alleged ravages of globalization, there are, as Patrick Macklem observes, 'multiple opportunities for holding corporations domestically accountable'. States can, for example, assert jurisdictions over local companies operating in other nations; revoke their charters; refuse to limit their liability in relation to foreign subsidiaries; condition access to markets on compliance with domestic standards; and participate in international regimes that demand promulgation and enforcement of domestic standards, thus deploying public international law to, in Macklem's words, 'rebuild . . . the state's capacity to regulate in the name of [social interests], multinational corporate power'.

> Rebuilding that capacity is neither simple nor easy. In the developed world, political inertia and corporate influence work against states, creating robust extra-territorial jurisdictions over the corporations they create and enable . . . In the developing world, and often the developed world too, regulatory laws and regimes can be poorly conceived, under-enforced, corrupted, and unduly influenced by industry. As in every other area of human endeavour, a gap exists here between actual practice and ideal possibility. Building

---

8 See George Monbiot, TTIP may be dead, but a worse trade deal is coming, *The Guardian*, 7 September 2016, on which this paragraph draws.

effective public and democratic governance of the global economy is what is needed to narrow that gap, a project requiring much work both domestically and internationally.

The private regulation movement effectively abandons that project, prescribing instead alternatives to public and democratic governance that elevates market values and actors to governing status. The result is to make regulation an 'adjunct to the market', in Polyani's words, and thus to create a global economy in which 'social relations . . . [are] embedded in the economic system' rather than the 'economy . . . embedded in social relations'. As this Article has argued, the case for private regulation is unconvincing because it depends upon ignoring, thereby making invisible, the real and robust role law plays in enabling and protecting MNCs. Bringing that role to light is important not only for revealing the true and disturbing vision underlying private regulation – a world where public power promotes private interests, while public interest depends on private power for protection – but also for making visible the urgent need and many possibilities for finding better ways forward. (Bakan, 2015, pp. 299–300, emphasis in the original)

Thus, more effective monitoring and regulation is required of the activities of multinational corporations – from their effects on the environment to their attempts to avoid and evade taxation. That requires national governments to work together to this end. Alongside this, promoting a healthy degree of corporate diversity is also vital to the success of any economy. It may be that member-owned companies such as co-operatives, mutuals and employee-owned firms are less suited to operating multinationally. Similarly, despite the UK government's relaxed attitude to handing vital parts of its national economic infrastructure to the public sectors of other countries, it may be that most countries would never do this to such an extent, and that public ownership is likewise generally limited in its multinational scope. These corporate forms – member and public ownership – may be less likely to pursue globalisation than are shareholder-owned firms. If so, this might be seen as representing an additional benefit, rather than being a hardship, in fostering local and regional economic activity. Promoting localisation in place of uber-globalisation.

6   The practice of globalisation

'Take back control!'
(Slogan of the 2016 campaign for the UK to leave the EU)

The practice of globalisation has proven to be more complex and varied than the theory might have suggested. Thus, for example, Goldberg and Pavcnik (2007) report that:

> One of the few uncontroversial insights of trade theory is that changes in a country's exposure to international trade, and world markets more generally, affect the distribution of resources within the country . . . What is . . . surprising is that the distributional changes went in the opposite direction from the one suggested by conventional wisdom: while globalisation was expected to help the less skilled who are presumed to be the locally relatively abundant factor in developing countries, there is overwhelming evidence that these are generally not better off, at least not relative to workers with higher skill or educational levels. What explains this. . .?

> First, the exposure of developing countries to international markets. . . has increased substantially. Second. . . all existing measures for inequality in developing countries seem to point to an increase in inequality (Goldberg and Pavcnik, 2007, pp. 39-40)

They conclude that there are a variety of causal mechanisms at work, and these have varied across countries and over time, depending amongst other things on the exact institutional and other arrangements in place at the time:

> From a policy point of view, this implies that attempts to alleviate the potentially adverse distributional effect of globalisation in the short or medium run need to be grounded in a careful study of the nature of globalisation and the individual circumstances in each country. (Goldberg and Pavcnik, 2007, p. 41)

For those of us who regard the economy as both inherently complex and continually changing, and who expect economic developments to be heavily dependent on historical, institutional, cultural, social and political factors, such a conclusion comes as no surprise. There are, certainly, things that can be done – not least, because each and every one of the preceding list of determining factors can themselves be influenced and changed. However, it does mean that the indicative policy ideas referred to in subsequent chapters are just that – indicative; the actual policies appropriate to any given economy will depend on the specifics of that economy, and these in turn will change over time. Indeed, one of the important messages of the research reported in this book is that despite globalisation, it is certainly *not* the case that a single global economy has been created, which can be acted upon with policies designed and implemented at the global level alone. Quite the contrary, the nation state remains the most important institutional arrangement for delivering policy, not only for their own economies, but also in co-operation with others for the global economy.

6.1   Capitalism unleashed

As discussed in Chapter 2, the nature of globalisation changed with the Thatcher and Reagan governments of the 1980s, ideologically committed to free-market capitalism, given free rein after the collapse of the Soviet Union. The resulting 'capitalism unleashed' led to repeated financial and economic crises across the globe. (Laeven and Valencia (2008) report that between 1970 and 2007, the International Monetary Fund recorded 124 systemic bank crises, 208 currency crises and 63 sovereign debt crises.) The Asian financial crisis of 1998 led to the IMF demanding austerity policies as a requirement for assistance, which most of the countries affected accepted – to their cost. Malaysia declined, and instead imposed capital controls, which were totally alien to the Washington Consensus. In the event, the Malaysian option proved the more appropriate. (For an analysis of the Asian financial crisis, and a discussion of the Malaysian versus the orthodox approaches, see Michie, 1999.) The criticism of the IMF for having advocated their austerity measures led to the organisation establishing an 'Independent Evaluation Office' (IEO) to undertake assessments of its policies and programmes, after the event. This IEO undertook an evaluation of the IMF's role in Europe during the post-2008 crisis, in particular of the financing arrangements that the IMF concluded with the 'euro area' members, namely the 2010 Stand-By Arrangement with Greece, the 2010 Extended Arrangement with Ireland, and the 2011 Extended Arrangement with Portugal. (For a report, analysis and discussion of the Greek crisis, including the role of the IMF and the other international bodies involved, see the account by Galbraith (2016), tellingly entitled *Welcome to the Poisoned Chalice*.)[1] This IMF (IEO) report admitted that:

> The IMF. . . did not foresee the magnitude of the risks that would later become paramount. The IMF . . . along with most other experts, missed the build-up of banking system risks in some countries. In general, the IMF shared the widely-held 'Europe is different' mindset that encouraged the view that large imbalances in national current accounts were little cause for concern. . .

> The IMF-supported programs in Greece and Portugal incorporated overly optimistic growth projections. More realistic projections would have made clear the likely impact of fiscal consolidation on growth and debt dynamics (IEO, 2016, p. vii, Executive Summary).[2]

There are two important points here about the nature of globalisation. First, the reality was not about creating a 'global economy' – a large part of the process was about capital movements within the EU, and within the North American Free Trade Area (NAFTA), and of course between the two. Second, the nature of those institutional blocks – the EU and NAFTA – was very much along the free-market, 'capitalism unleashed' agenda.

> The implementation in 1994 of the NAFTA, building on the earlier framework of the 1989 Canada–US FTA, marked a watershed in the historical political-economic evolution of Canada and Mexico. Political and business elites in both countries abandoned earlier attempts to forge more nationalist, proactive development strategies, and instead embarked on a course of closer integration with the US market, and the US model of political-economy. The NAFTA had less dramatic, though still important, effects in the US. The relatively simple task of eliminating tariffs on intra-NAFTA merchandise trade constitutes a modest portion of the overall NAFTA package. More important has been the NAFTA's attempt to

---

1 Reading the proceedings reminded me, though, of the account from Lord Krebs of taking up the job as head of the UK's Food Standards Agency and being told by the British politician Frank Dobson that he couldn't understand why Krebs had accepted the job: 'People say it's a poisoned chalice, but I can't see the chalice anywhere' (private correspondence).

2 For a discussion of this report, see Eichengreen (2016).

establish a continent-wide regime of deregulated, market-oriented economic development. Indeed, the Mexican government's primary interest in the NAFTA may have been precisely to commit itself publicly and permanently to a broadly neoliberal development strategy, thus winning the confidence and approval of both international investors and domestic wealth-holders. The NAFTA has had a significant impact on trade and direct investment flows within North America, but the overall impact of NAFTA on aggregate economic variables (such as investment, growth, productivity and incomes) has been disappointing, including for Mexico (which was expected by economists to benefit dramatically from its integration within the continental market). The prospects for the expansion of NAFTA (to include other countries in the Western Hemisphere), or for its deepening (to address topics such as monetary integration or migration) seem dim. Meanwhile, the broader relative decline of the US economy (most dramatically visible in the financial crisis and recession of 2009) has imposed spillover consequences on its NAFTA partners, and on the long-run vitality of the continental market generally. Without a substantial revitalization of both North American economic leadership, and initiatives to further intensify and deepen economic links between the three NAFTA partners, it would seem that NAFTA's long-run economic and political importance is likely to fade. (Stanford, 2011, pp. 351–352)

To the extent that globalisation has involved US companies and capital moving beyond NAFTA and the EU, Craypo and Wilkinson (2011) warn that it threatens to undermine what in many cases have been effective productive systems and development strategies in those other countries, which instead are forced down the US free-market cul-de-sac:

It is also argued that the relocation of production out of the US merely reflects the comparative advantage of developing countries in the price of low-skilled labour (Wood, 1994). But . . . labour migration and job emigration now affects all grades of workers and the driving force of labour immigration and job emigration is tapping sources of low pay whatever the level of skill. Moreover, it is not altogether clear how the immiseration of a large proportion of the US population benefits world development even if jobs are created elsewhere. And, there must be a question of the overall effect on jobs as the lowering of pay relative to productivity to enhance profits reduces the capability of the world's workers to consume what they produce and therefore the overall level of effective demand. There can be no doubt that the transfer of technological enterprise accompanying the global activity of US corporations has advantages for other countries but this is offset by its destructive capabilities. But the greater threat to the world economic order is the globalisation of corporate liberalism, the dominant ideology of the US productive system, with its insistence on low-wage and *flexible* labour markets, reduced levels of welfare provision and of unrestricted corporate activity, however exploitative and destructive that might be. As a consequence, despite the superior economic performance of the productive systems that lead in establishing the comparative advantages of high road competitive strategies, they are currently being pressed to move to the low road by deregulating their labour, product and financial markets to free-up their corporate sectors. How this propels them down the route pioneered by the US will determine the extent to which they replicate that productive system's poverty, inequality and operational and dynamic inefficiencies. (Craypo and Wilkinson, 2011, p. 375)

The free-market 'capitalism unleashed' form of globalisation was also pursued through the General Agreement on Trade in Services (GATS):

The GATS strictly limits the pursuit of more progressive and egalitarian forms of social reproduction while privileging the interests of private capital, chiefly transnational service corporations, and their goal of accumulation. Although multilateral negotiations to broaden and deepen the GATS, launched in 2001 in Doha have faltered, the legal framework pioneered by the GATS continues to expand through the proliferation of bilateral trade and investment agreements. Ironically, the high levels of public debt incurred to stabilise financial capital during the recent crisis will likely be used to justify a new wave of global restructuring of public services characterised by privatisation, outsourcing and increased corporate provision of publicly funded basic services. The constitutional role of the GATS in shaping this restructuring to serve global corporate interests raises such serious challenges to democratic governance and social cohesion that it is certain to stimulate further public interest and controversy. (Sinclair, 2011, pp. 430–431)

6.2   The practice of globalisation since 2007

The free-market 'capitalism unleashed' form of globalisation from the 1980s onwards led to a series of financial and economic crises around the world, culminating in the 2007–2008 international financial crisis and the subsequent 2009 global recession, together sometimes referred to as 'the Great Recession' (following the Great Depression of the

1930s).[3] What marked the Great Recession out from all other recessions since the Second World War is that for the first time (since the Great Depression of the 1930s), the global output and income of the world taken as a whole actually fell. (In previous recessions, output and income fell in some countries but such losses were more than offset by growth elsewhere.) Since then there has been an additional uniqueness of the Great Recession, as compared to all previous recessions, namely the weak recovery. At the time of writing in 2017 most economies have experienced a 'lost decade'. The current recovery from the Great Recession is actually weaker than was the recovery from the Great Depression – although perhaps not surprisingly, as there was more positive action taken in the 1930s. Thus, for example:

> From 2005 to 2014, the real income of two-thirds of households in 25 developed economies was flat or fell. Only after very aggressive government intervention in taxes and transfers have some countries been able to hold families at least even. (Tyson and Mendonca, 2016)

Similarly:

> Large segments of the population in advanced countries have not been doing well: in the US, the bottom 90% has endured income stagnation for a third of a century. Median income for full-time male workers is actually *lower* in real (inflation-adjusted) terms than it was 42 years ago. At the bottom, real wages are comparable to their level 60 years ago.

> Branko Milanovic's new book *Global Inequality: A New Approach for the Age of Globalization* provides some vital insights, looking at the big winners and losers in terms of income over the two decades from 1988 to 2008. Among the big winners were the global 1%, the world's plutocrats, but also the middle class in newly emerging economies. Among the big losers – those who gained little or nothing – were those at the bottom and the middle and working classes in the advanced countries. Globalization is not the only reason, but it is one of the reasons. (Stiglitz, 2016b)

These effects came under the spotlight in the UK following the 2016 referendum vote to leave the EU, and the question had to be faced as

---

3 Eichengreen (2015) provides a detailed comparative analysis of the Great Depression of the 1930s and the Great Recession of 2008–2009, arguing that the history of the Great Depression shaped how policy makers perceived and responded to the international financial crisis of 2007–2008 and the subsequent Great Recession of 2009.

to why the majority had voted against, despite having been told that membership was economically advantageous – usually a killer argument in elections. Faced with this question, an analysis of the data suggested that while it may indeed have been economically advantageous to some, and indeed to the country on average, these advantages were by no means spread equally across the country, either geographically or across social classes. Quite the contrary, the only two areas of the UK in which GDP per head had returned to its pre-2007–2008 financial crisis levels almost ten years later in 2016 were London and the southeast:

> In all other parts of the UK, GDP has not recovered. For example, in Northern Ireland, it is still more than 10% below its peak, and in Yorkshire and Humberside more than 5% below.

> If we turn from income to wealth, the picture is much the same.

> Over recent years, there have been fairly rapid rises in UK asset prices – houses, shares and bonds. These have increased measured national wealth by as much as £2.7 trillion since 2009. This is quite a financial harvest, helped by the stimulus provided by the world's central banks. But the distribution has been far from even across the regions. The largest wealth gains by households since 2008 have been in London (almost 50%) and the southeast (25%). Elsewhere, the gains have been far smaller, and in some regions wealth has fallen.

> As many as half of all British households have had no increase in their take-home pay since 2005, once adjusted for inflation. This is the longest period of wage stagnation since at least the middle of the 19th century. The majority of British households have faced a lost decade of income.

> The pattern of wealth gains across rich and poor households is even more striking. All of the large gains in recent years have been harvested by the asset-rich. The wealth of the richest 20% of households has risen by nearly 20% since 2010 . . . Meanwhile, the wealth of the poorest 20% of households has fallen by about 20% over the same period. (Haldane, 2016)

Thus, for those not enjoying increased wealth, being told that 'the country' is becoming wealthier may make things worse, not better; it may make those voters more alienated than if they thought everyone was in the same boat, and the situation was no good for any of them.[4]

---

4 Nolan et al. (2016) document the causes of household incomes falling behind GDP per capita, demonstrating that some but not most are due to increased inequality (falling family size being the

And for the EU and 'Brexit' (the acronym for Britain exiting the EU), read globalisation. Indeed, many UK voters may have seen the EU and globalisation as one and the same thing – a process whereby the free-market and big business seemed to be given pride of place; national sovereignty was given over either to that free-market and those big businesses, or to 'super national' bodies, or both; and where it was claimed that this was bringing great prosperity to the country, and yet for many, they seemed to be missing out.[5]

Lanchester (2016) provides a fascinating analysis of the issues around the referendum, but it could just have easily been written on the issues around globalisation:

> To be born in many places in Britain is to suffer an irreversible lifelong defeat – a truncation of opportunity, of education, of access to power, of life expectancy. . . . This new work doesn't do what the old work did: it doesn't offer a sense of identity or community or self-worth. The word 'precarious' has as its underlying sense 'depending on the favour of another person'. Somebody can take away the things you have whenever they feel like it. The precariat, as the new class is called, might not know the etymology, but it doesn't need to: the reality is all too familiar. . . .

> There was no strategy to replace the lost industry; that was left to the free-market. With these policies, parts of the country have simply been left behind. The white working class is correct to feel abandoned: it has been. No political party has anything to offer it except varying levels of benefits. The people in the rich parts of the country pay the taxes which support the poor parts. . . . It's a system bitterly resented both by the beneficiaries and by the suppliers of the largesse. . . .

> If I had to pick one sentence I've heard more than any other in the last six years of conversation about economics, it would be 'Why aren't people more angry?' The Brexit vote showed that plenty of them are. But perhaps it expressed that other feeling, the one of bewilderment, just as much. 'Take back control' is a cynical but extremely astute pitch to an electorate in that state of mind. (Lanchester, 2016, p. 4)

---

most important); but as indicated above, there is also the problem of GDP per capita growth being unequally shared geographically as well as across income bands, and also the growth in inequality has been even greater when looking at wealth than it has been when looking at income.

5 For an analysis of the 'left behind' working class white voters in the north of England, who were an important factor in the anti-EU referendum result, and would tend to express similarly anti-globalisation attitudes, see for example Goodwin and Ford (2013).

According to research by the McKinsey Global Institute, across the 25 leading economies, 500 million people suffered from flat or falling pay in the decade from 2005 to 2014, covering the 2007–2008 global financial crisis and the Great Recession of 2009. In Italy, 97 per cent of households saw their incomes fall or remain stagnant, 80 per cent in the US, 70 per cent in the UK and the Netherlands, 63 per cent in France, and 20 per cent in Sweden.[6]

Globally, world trade grew at an average of 6 per cent a year from 1980 to 2008; between 2009 and 2016 that growth rate was halved, reflecting both the Great Recession and the weak recovery. (IMF, 2016)

6.3   The precariat[7]

Waters and Chan (2016) analyse the apparent increase in suicides amongst workers, linked to increased stress and intensification of work, which they ascribe in large part to globalisation:

> Workplace suicides are sharply on the rise internationally, with increasing numbers of employees choosing to take their own lives in the face of extreme pressures at work. Recent studies in the United States, Australia, Japan, South Korea, China, India and Taiwan all point to a steep rise in suicides in the context of a generalised deterioration in working conditions.

> Rising suicides are part of the profound transformations in the workplace that have taken place over the past 30 years. These transformations are arguably rooted in the political and economic shift to globalisation that has radically altered the way we work.

> . . . today's globalised workplace is characterised by job insecurity, intense work, forced redeployments, flexible contracts, worker surveillance, and limited social protection and representation. Zero-hour contracts are the new norm for many. . .

> Workers move in and out of jobs which give little meaning to their lives. This shift has had deleterious effects on many people's experience of work,

6 See Elliott (2016).

7 For Standing (2011, 2014), the 'precariat' is the new social class of the 21st century, characterised by a lack of security; see guystanding.com.

with rising cases of acute stress, anxiety, sleep disorders, burnout, hopeless-
ness and, in some cases, suicide.

6.4 Conclusion

The gap between the theory and practice of economics has been
referred to above, and is returned to in subsequent chapters. A key
failing is to find that in theory, losers from policy change can be compensated by the winners, leaving everyone better off – and then to find
that on the basis of that rationale, the policy has been implemented,
but without compensating the losers. Thus, in relation to globalisation:

> While seemingly elegant in theory, globalization suffers in practice. . . .
> Those who worship at the altar of free trade – including me – must come to
> grips with this glaring disconnect.
>
> The design of more enlightened policies must account for the powerful pres-
> sures now bearing down on a much broader array of workers. The hyper-
> speed of Globalization 2.0 suggests the need for quicker triggers and wider
> coverage for worker retraining, relocation allowances, job-search assistance,
> wage insurance for older workers, and longer-duration unemployment
> benefits.
>
> As history cautions, the alternative – whether it is Brexit or America's new
> isolationism – is an accident waiting to happen. It is up to those of us
> who defend free trade and globalization to prevent that, by offering con-
> crete solutions that address the very real problems that now afflict so many
> workers. (Roach, 2016)

A second failing is that mainstream economics assumes that markets
tend towards equilibrium. There is no logical basis for this in theory,
and no evidence in practice. A more realistic, appropriate and useful
economics needs to draw upon the rich heritage from, and vibrant
current research into, institutional, evolutionary, and complexity
economics. That might sound like a confusing list, but it basically
means recognising that institutions matter, that we learn over time
from experience, that both these sets of factors affect our behaviour,
and that the outcomes are thus complex. Pretty obvious, and simple,
actually.[8]

---

8 For a discussion of such an approach, see for example Silim (2016).

7   The global architecture

> I was brought up, like most Englishmen, to respect free trade not only as
> an economic doctrine which a rational and an instructed person could not
> doubt but also as a part of the moral law. I regarded departures from it as
> being at the same time an imbecility and an outrage.
> (John Maynard Keynes, National Self-Sufficiency, 1933, *The New Statesman*
> (UK) and *The Yale Review* (US))

Chapter 2, on the historical context of globalisation, reported on the
marked contrast in the process of globalisation between two successive periods: 1914–1945 was an era of world wars, hyperinflation in
some countries and unsustainable speculative booms in others, the
1929 Wall Street Crash followed by the Great Depression of the 1930s,
and the rise of Nazism in Germany, Militarism in Japan, and Fascism
in Italy, Spain and Portugal. The subsequent Golden Age of Capitalism
from 1945 to 1975 saw an era of global growth and development, with
a commitment to full employment. That the second era was more successful than the first was no accident. It was the result of deliberate
design and policy action. Put simply, at the start of the first, unhappy
era, Keynes had warned, in his *Economic Consequences of the Peace*,
that the proposed policy agenda was folly, indeed disastrous, and that
no good would come of it. He warned again that Winston Churchill's
attempt to put Britain back on the gold standard would be disastrous.
Again, he was ignored, and again he was proved right.

But in 1936 Keynes published his *General Theory*, explaining what
caused recession and unemployment, and what could be done to
avoid and if necessary tackle it. His aim in writing the book was to
change the way people thought about economics, and so it proved
(outside the UK Treasury, of course). It meant he could no longer be
ignored. So when the Second World War broke out, his *How to Pay
for the War* (1940) was influential. And when it came to the post-war
discussions on what global architecture should be put in place to
avoid any return to the previous era, to avoid any 'return to the 30s',

Keynes led the delegation for the British. They managed to get agreement on new institutions – the International Monetary Fund and the World Bank, and on new international monetary arrangements around fixed exchange rates underpinned by a new gold standard linked to the US dollar.

This international architecture, combined with domestic commitments to full employment, increased living standards, and a welfare state was an important stabilising and confidence-enhancing backdrop to that era of reasonably steady growth and development. Keynes's proposals were not, however, accepted in full – and this made the arrangements more prone to the difficulties encountered in the 1970s, and thus more vulnerable to ideological attack from the monetarists.

This attack was led by Milton Freidman, who advocated a free-market, laissez-faire policy domestically and globally. Domestically he was in favour of deregulation. When debating on British TV in 1980 he was asked whether it would not be sensible to regulate to prevent companies producing drugs like thalidomide, to which he replied that regulation wasn't required, since the bad press from the damage done would cause a fall in the company's share price, which would prevent that or any other company from repeating such behaviour. Globally, he argued similarly against regulation or any other barriers to free trade, arguing that Japan and other successful economies had been successful because of such free-market policies. The Cambridge economist Robert (Bob) Rowthorn pointed out – in their TV debate – that this was utter nonsense, and was indeed the exact opposite of the truth. Japan and every other successful industrial economy had developed behind protective tariff walls, and with a host of measures to support their domestic industries to develop.

The current arrangements might look superficially to be similar to the Golden Age arrangements as advocated by Keynes, in the sense that the IMF and World Bank remain in place, but while their names continue, their outlook and policy changed along with the 1980s Thatcher/Reagan shift from Keynes to Friedman. The IMF and World Bank came to advocate and indeed impose the new laissez-faire ideology. And crucially, controls on the movement of speculative capital were removed, allowing funds to slosh around the globe in search of a quick killing, regardless of whether such action was conducive to economic progress or not.

So, where do we go from here, in terms of appropriate international arrangements for a new era? First, as argued above, the status quo is not an option – we need a Green New Deal, and a new global architecture to deliver it. Second, much of the change currently being promoted would move us still further down the disastrous 'capitalism unleashed' cul-de-sac that delivered the mess that we're currently in – such as the proposed Trans-Pacific Partnership (TPP) between the US and eleven Pacific Rim countries, the Transatlantic Trade and Investment Partnership (TTIP) between the EU and the US, and the Canada–EU Comprehensive Economic and Trade Agreement (CETA).[1]

7.1   A new global architecture[2]

The complete game changer is climate change, and the threat it poses to the whole of humanity. That must take centre stage in any new arrangements. Whether that can be done by making climate change the central requirement for the IMF and World Bank to address in their programmes and activities, or whether it requires a new institution, either alongside or in place of one or both of those is, I think, an open question.[3] But however it is delivered, tackling climate change needs to be the fundamental goal around which all else must fit.

Beyond tackling climate change, as for the macroeconomic stabilisation and other activities of the IMF and World Bank, these need to not just revert from the capitalism unleashed, Milton Friedman laissez-faire approach of the past 30 years, to the Keynesian approach of the Golden Age era,[4] but they should go further than this, and recreate the sort of arrangements which Keynes would have liked to have seen put in place in 1945, had the American negotiators not blocked them. This means that when the global economy is in danger of slipping into recession due to imbalances in trade across the globe, the onus

1   For a discussion of which, see Barker (2016). Sinclair et al. (2016) argue that CETA would have problematic impacts on public services, domestic regulation, intellectual property rights, and government measures to address climate change.

2   For a detailed analysis of the key issues, see the various contributors to Michie and Grieve Smith (1999).

3   For a discussion of the roles of the IMF and World Bank, and their possible reform, see for example Toye (2011).

4   And the IMF has at least published a piece entitled 'Neoliberalism: Oversold?' (Ostry et al., 2016), although they might have done without the question mark; or even renamed the piece: 'Problems with Neoliberalism: Oversold, Over Hyped, and Over Here'.

should be on the surplus economies to expand so that their consumers buy more from abroad, thus eliminating their surpluses and hence the imbalances.[5]

One of the most damaging free-market policies from the Thatcher, Reagan, and Friedman era of laissez-faire was abolishing controls on speculative money flows across borders. By speculative I mean flows which aren't required for any genuine economic purpose – to finance trade, or build factories overseas, or for tourists to spend abroad. These genuine purposes for moving currencies across borders had always been permitted. What has proved destabilising is to have removed the controls on the movement of funds for all other, speculative purposes.

7.2   Controlling global capital flows

During the Golden Age of Capitalism, almost all successful economies had strict controls in place on the international movement of capital. The principle was that capital movement across borders was permitted only for purposes such as tourism, trade, or investment in productive assets – that is, for purposes other than just speculation, the purpose of which was simply the financial gain of the speculators. That principle was abandoned by the Thatcher government in 1979, wedded as it was to Milton Friedman's picture of free-market capitalism, followed by other countries as the whole global system of capital controls unravelled. A new global architecture would need to include controls on such speculative flows – like adding buffers to a tray full of water, to prevent the water flowing in an uncontrolled way. While the ability to impose actual restraints would at the very least need to be held in reserve, a large part of the job might be done through introducing a tax on such speculative movements, which would have the dual effect of reducing such activity, which would be good for the stability of the global economy, and, to the extent that such activity was not thereby completely eliminated, would deliver additional tax revenues, which might be used to fund sustainability projects globally – a Green New Deal. (Such a 'transactions' tax – sometimes referred to as a 'Robin Hood' tax – is discussed in Chapter 9.)

---

5   For a discussion of both the shortcomings of globalisation, and of the need to reform the global institutions, see Stiglitz (2002).

7.3   Free trade or fair trade?

DeMartino (2011) sets out a comprehensive proposal for regulating international trade along lines that would be fair to all parties, and sympathetic to and supportive of sustainable development – as opposed to free trade which is often anything but. (Meaning, often not sympathetic to and supportive of sustainable development, and often not 'free' in any meaningful sense of that term).

> In my own work (2000) and in joint work with Stephen Cullenberg (DeMartino and Cullenberg, 1994) I have advanced a new multilateral approach to trade policy, called the Social Index Tariff Structure (SITS) regime, which would penalise countries for pursuing advantage based on weak standards through social tariffs, while substantially rewarding those countries that take steps to promote worker rights (and human development more generally) through subsidies funded by the social tariffs. . . .
>
> Contrary to the view of most neoclassical economists, global neo-liberalism is not the best imaginable economic system. It is inducing extraordinary inequality, and it threatens to deepen that inequality in the future. Today it is proving to be unsustainable, owing to the insecurity, crises, political backlash and ecological degradation that it is inducing. (DeMartino, 2011, pp. 492–493)

The 'Fair Trade Movement' has similar goals. Importantly, that movement is not just about trying to ensure that a fair price is paid in any trade today, but also about trying to assist the producers to organise collectively through producer co-operatives, so that they will be in a better position to try to negotiate appropriate prices in the future, on a sustainable basis, even in the absence of interventions such as from the Fair Trade Movement. (For a detailed discussion of the Fair Trade Movement, see Nicholls and Huybrechts, 2017.)

7.4   Globalisation and labour standards

Wood (1998) analyses the impact of globalisation on labour market inequalities in developed countries, finding negative impacts on the employment and wages of unskilled workers; and Wood (1994, Chapter 9) discusses similar effects within developing countries. However, Singh and Zammit (2011, p. 252, note 11) point out that Wood's estimates of the extent of the impact 'far exceed those of other economists'.[6] There have for many years been calls for the adoption of minimum labour standards globally, both to protect those who might otherwise not receive those minimum standards – whether those be economic (most obviously pay rates), or freedom from child labour or slavery (legal), or some minimum health and safety standards (regulatory) – and also to prevent those workers who do currently enjoy those minimum standards, at least, from being undercut by others who don't – in other words, to create a level playing field where the good employers aren't undercut by the bad, with the bad in turn being undercut by the very worst. (For a review of the literature on globalisation and labour, analysing the impact of globalisation on employment, distribution of income and labour standards, see Lee, 1997.)

Singh and Zammit (2011) warn against such an approach for fear that it be used by those in the developed countries as a disguised form of protectionism against those in the developing countries, by imposing standards which would make the developing countries uncompetitive. However, they do argue that certain minimum standards – such as prohibiting slavery, for example – do need to be imposed and enforced. But beyond this, they see the key aim as being the sustainable development of all societies, for which the most important policy agenda is not to impose minimum standards, as to pursue international co-operative policies to encourage balanced and sustainable development, so that labour standards can be gradually raised across the globe:

> Recent evidence suggests that labour standards in both China and India have improved as a result of local labour pressures, as well as the structural change brought about by government policies promoting fast economic growth. Hundreds of millions of rural workers in both countries have found work in the cities. Their labour standards may be expected to improve, as in the case of East Asian countries in the 1980s and 1990s, when labour standards improved rapidly in tandem with the increasing demand for non-agricultural labour. At the same time, economic growth in China and India has, inter alia, increased demand for imports from the US and elsewhere and hence reduced US financial deficits.

> However, as Izurieta and Singh (2010) point out, fast growth in India and China is not an unalloyed good for the US economy and its workers. These

---

6 Brown and Lauder (1996) also criticise the literature that emphasises the need to upgrade educational standards whilst failing to address the problem that a polarised society will not create high standards of educational achievement for all.

countries' growth entails increased demand for imported energy and other raw materials, pushing world commodity prices sky high. Their simulation analysis based on an econometric model of the world economy suggests that fast Indian growth at 9 per cent per annum and Chinese growth at 10 per cent per annum is not compatible with a full employment level of growth of 3 per cent a year in the US. Were the US to have full employment growth, India and China could only grow at less than their desired rates of growth. The Izurieta and Singh analysis indicates that this conflict of interest can only be resolved by means of close cooperation between the three countries in energy conservation and environmental measures. Such a scenario will inevitably benefit labour markets and standards in both rich and poor countries particularly in the medium and long term. The full potential of globalisation in terms of improved labour standards and decent work can only be achieved if there is greater policy coordination between nation states. Globalisation left only to market forces cannot deliver worldwide full employment or decent livelihoods for the entire workforce. (Singh and Zammit, 2011, pp. 250–251)

The debates around labour standards are analysed in detail by Heintz (2011), who summarises the key arguments in support of global labour standards, evaluates the threat of negative consequences that could spring from such regulations, and discusses current possible developments in implementation strategies. Following a detailed analysis and discussion, he concludes that the limitations of any scheme to introduce global labour standards need to be recognised, including that:

Most significantly, only a subset of the world's workforce would receive any benefits, since the standards are aimed at workers who produce goods for export. Workers producing non-traded goods and services would not be directly affected by interventions such as a standardized code of conduct or a social clause. In these cases, the ongoing mission of the ILO to encourage states to implement and enforce better domestic standards remains invaluable. Furthermore, adopting expansionary macroeconomic policies could be more strategic for improving the well-being of all workers than a targeted set of labour standards. A coordinated approach involving a range of interventions – both macroeconomic and in terms of international regulation – would also reduce the tensions between better standards and job creation.

Despite the limitations of global labour standards, the potential that such interventions have for improving the working lives of a significant number of people should not be underestimated. Furthermore, the possible impact of such a system extends well beyond the benefits generated by its core policies.

The development of an appropriate regulatory scheme for enforcing basic standards of decency could serve as a model for governing multinational economic activities more generally. Because of these possible contributions, striving to create an effective framework for global labour standards represents an important policy goal in this era of the new international division of labour. (Heintz, 2011, pp. 270–271)

7.5   Migration

The issue of how best to regulate international labour migration is discussed and set out well and comprehensively by Ruhs (2013). Two difficult debates that he confronts are those over whether there should be free, unrestricted migration, and second, whether migrants should be eligible to full rights once they arrive in their new country of residence. His research finds that these two factors are negatively correlated; that is, where there are no restrictions on migration, the migrants are typically given fewer rights, whereas when migrants are given full rights, their entry tends to be restricted. Ruhs therefore concludes that this trade-off should be recognised, and it should be accepted that whilst some rights need to be recognised from day one, others (such as the right to vote in elections) might not be awarded until after some passage of time, since such an approach is likely to lead to countries permitting higher rates of migration than would otherwise be the case, which he takes to be a good thing, other things being equal.[7]

7.6   International development

The International Monetary Fund (IMF) in 2016 recognised that some of its previous advice to developing economies had been counterproductive, in terms of enabling their development. There are many examples of the IMF, World Bank and others imposing damaging economic conditions on developing economies – not quite on the scale of the reparations payments imposed after 1918 on Germany, but with damaging effects on the ability of those economies to develop, nonetheless.

Michie and Padayachee (1998) detail the example of post-apartheid South Africa, where the early hopes for the post-apartheid era led to disappointingly weak transformation, low growth, persistently high

---

7   See also his further discussion, and response to critics, in Ruhs (2016a, 2016b).

unemployment, and a continuation of the huge imbalance in income and wealth between the white and black populations, notwithstanding the enrichment of a small proportion of the black population. Amongst the seven key factors that facilitated the ANC's conversion from a radical strategy of reconstruction and development to an essentially free-market one, was that:

> [T]he international financial institutions, including the IMF and World Bank, together with Western governments, have been an influence over ANC economic thinking since the 1990s. However, theirs has been a successful exercise in moral suasion (or indirect lobbying), for neither of the Bretton Woods organisations has had much direct leverage (via loan conditionality) over the direction of ANC economic policy since 1994 (Padayachee, 1997, p. 50). (Michie and Padayachee, 1998, p. 633)[8]

The case of China is of course quite separate from other developing economies, given its size and economic success, but for an interesting analysis of its future prospects, including as regards societal innovativeness, see Redding and Drew (2016). On Eastern Europe, and the impact of the politics of globalisation, see for example Deacon (2000).

7.7   Industrial sectors

Most industrial sectors are today hugely global in their organisation, structure and ownership. The auto-industry might be thought to be an obvious example. However, Bailey et al. (2010, p. 313) argue that:

> Overall, what can be seen in the industry so far is not so much globalization, as really regionalization within a global pattern, whereby the original equipment manufacturers (OEMs) assemble and design vehicles locally, close to the customer (witness major OEMs setting up design studios in China and India for example). A key question then centres on whether the emergence of China and India as major producers and exporters will challenge this pattern, given the possibility of low labour costs and economies of scale overcoming transportation costs to major markets. Whilst the OEMs currently prefer to locate near the final market, they have shifted assembly operations towards low-cost central and Eastern Europe for example, within the EU.

---

8 For further analysis and discussion of the international constraints facing South Africa after apartheid, see Michie (1997), Michie and Padayachee (1997) and Harris and Michie (1998).

A new global architecture should make more coherent provision for such arrangements.

7.8   Global governance

On global governance, Lee (2011) argues that:

> In a departure from the capital controls and managed exchange rate regime of the post-war Bretton Woods international economic order, national governments have increasingly adopted the economic policy prescriptions of the dominant neoliberal orthodoxy of the 'Washington Consensus' (Williamson, 1993). This American model for reconciling national economic policy choices with globalisation has prescribed the pursuit of monetary stability and fiscal prudence, with budget deficits small enough to be financed without extra taxation; the establishment of priorities in public expenditure through a transfer of resources from politically sensitive areas, such as welfare payments, towards neglected fields with high economic returns, such as investment in tangible and intangible infrastructure; and tax reforms to broaden the tax base and cut marginal tax rates to provide incentives. Despite the repeated promise of a dividend of macroeconomic stability and higher rates of economic growth, the 'Washington Consensus' has actually delivered slower growth. During the inflationary and recession-ridden 1970s, annual world output growth had increased by 4.4 per cent, but this duly declined to only 3.4 per cent during the 1980s in the era of Thatcherism and Reaganomics. Following the collapse of communism and the further rolling forward of the frontiers of the market, during the 1990s, world output growth had barely averaged 3.0 per cent (IMF, 1999: 2, 27).
> (Lee, 2011, p. 409)

Against this, Lee considers the attempt to replace the 'Washington Consensus' model of global governance with the 'third way' espoused by President Clinton and Prime Minister Blair, concluding that:

> However, just as the third way Clinton administration in the US had misinterpreted the speculation- and consumer-led boom of the 'dotcom bubble' as the onset of 'a New Economy', characterised by *'extraordinary gains in performance – including rapid productivity growth, rising incomes, low unemployment, and moderate inflation'* (United States Government, 2001: 23; italics original), so too the transition from boom to bust, with the onset of a major financial crisis and the deepest recession since 1929, exposed New Labour's risk-based model of political economy as one

founded upon unsustainable debt and imprudence in public and private finances (Lee, 2009). (Lee, 2011, p. 417)

Lee (2011, p. 417) concludes that both models (the Washington Consensus and the 'third way') of global governance have failed, demonstrating 'that long-term stability in monetary and fiscal policy cannot be guaranteed in a world of liberalised financial markets and volatile short-term capital flows, without effective regulation (United Nations, 2009).'

In discussing what form such global regulatory governance needs to take, Koenig-Archibugi (2011) makes the point that:

> [T]he management of global affairs is not the preserve of governments, but involves a broad range of actors, at the domestic and transnational levels. Specifically, global governance implies that firms and NGOs are not simply the passive recipients of the rules negotiated by governments above their heads, but participate in various ways in the formulation of those rules through public-private partnerships, or even by establishing purely private regimes to regulate certain domains in their common interests. (Koenig-Archibugi, 2011, p. 399)

Similarly, Woodward (2011) argues that there are a multitude of structures and actors alongside states that:

> [P]ossess the power and authority to contribute to management of our collective affairs. There are many aspects of world politics, particularly in the ambit of security and military affairs, where the power and authority of states reigns supreme and where inter-state relations do largely explain outcomes. Equally, there are provinces where the authority of the state is contested, compromised or delegated and where the slack is picked up by structures of authority from beyond the state system. (Woodward, 2011, p. 390)

7.9   The global institutions

The global institutions and their roles are referred to in other chapters, but here we pull together the conclusions from those discussions, as to what roles they should play, which we would argue are as follows:

All international institutions need to focus on the need to *combat climate change*, but in this, the *World Bank* should take the lead, and this should be the prime purpose of the World Bank – to promote sustainable development, and tackle climate change.

The *International Monetary Fund* needs to be supportive of that agenda, but also needs to take the lead in re-establishing *control over global financial flows*. Electorates want to 'take back control', and rightly so. The IMF should work towards a new system of international capital controls that can act as a buffer to the unregulated sloshing around the global system of speculative funds, some of it no doubt derived from illegal tax evasion, and involved in drug trafficking and other such illegal activities. As discussed in Chapter 9, this should include a tax on such speculative capital movements.

Tax evasion and avoidance needs to be tackled properly and effectively. The illegal funds that have evaded tax – and which are therefore mostly either dormant or involved in funding other illegal activity – need to be returned to the regulated sector of the global economy and put to productive use. National governments need to co-operate over this, and the IMF and World Bank need to be supportive, but the *OECD* could be used to take the lead in this work, building on what they have already done.

The prime responsibility of the *United Nations*, along with supporting the ambitions regarding climate change, regulating financial flows, and tackling tax evasion, needs to be to seek to avoid armed conflict, and to seek the *peaceful resolution of conflicts*, if possible before they break out, but if necessary subsequently.

Of course, while the IMF has been claiming to have learned its lesson, that the austerity measures it imposed on struggling economies were, quite literally counterproductive, and while the other international institutions have been doing likewise to various degrees, some scepticism should remain as to how easy it would be to get these leopards to change their spots.

7.10   Conclusion: co-operation between nation states

There have been various contributions to the discussion on what a new global architecture needs to entail. Hirst and Thompson (1994), for example, suggested that such an approach should define, codify and guarantee the property rights of multinationals in their foreign direct investments; protect the rights of labour; recognise the rights of governments to defend certain of their legitimate national functions in respect of the economy; establish binding protocols on company taxation; establish a disputes mechanism that would be written into international law; and provide environmental protection. Rodrik (2016b) argues, in our view convincingly, that while climate change requires global co-operation because the planet has a single climate system, most economic policies relate to the relevant domestic economy first and foremost. So whilst some global governance is required, this should not distract us from the fact that domestic economic policies remain crucial.

> Whatever the original intentions, the performance of supernational or any other institutions depends on those who exercise effective control over them. Hence, in the absence of a global government, the failure of the Bretton Woods institutions to act in accordance with the principles that led to their creation stems not so much from the institutions themselves as from the attitude and policies of the governments of their dominant members. (Panic, 2011, p. 458)

Of course there is a huge amount of work needed to think through exactly what arrangements would be needed to deliver fully under all these areas, but crucial is to control capital flows, prioritise action to save and improve the environment, and to recast the IMF and World Bank economic programmes to support and promote sustainable development, rather than free-markets and austerity. The key point is for people to be actively engaged in seeking to tackle the problems and issues that face us all. Such involvement needs to be local and regional, through national governments, and *via* international organisations and institutions. In this it is important to recognise that national governments play a crucial role not only in national governance but also in influencing possibilities and outcomes at local, regional and global levels too.

8 Global challenges: conflict and terrorism; inequality; economic crises; and climate change

> Wealth is like muck. It is not good but if it be spread.
> (Francis Bacon, 17th century)[1]

The death of the nation state has been greatly exaggerated, repeatedly, and for several decades now. We do undoubtedly face various global challenges. But tackling them will require action at local, regional, national and global levels, and in each case, the role of nation states is crucial. An obvious such global issue would be flu pandemics that are no respecters of borders or nation states. Four other such phenomena which are discussed briefly in this chapter are conflict and terrorism; inequality; economic crises; and climate change. A fifth is taxation, which is discussed in Chapter 9.

8.1 Conflict and terrorism

Over the past fifteen years or so we appear to have witnessed a growth of global terrorism, and international conflict including wars. The two are related, most obviously with the terrorist attack on the 'twin towers' of the World Trade Centre on 11 September 2001 leading to the subsequent invasions of Afghanistan and Iraq, which led in turn to a growth in terrorism within those countries and their neighbouring states – and indeed globally. These developments might be regarded as somewhat ironic, as the supposed threat to world peace, namely the Soviet Union, ceased to exist in 1991, and Fukuyama had already in 1989 – with the Soviet Union clearly struggling – declared 'The End of History':

> What we may be witnessing is not just the end of the Cold War, or the passing of a particular period of post-war history, but the end of history as such: that is, the end point of mankind's ideological evolution and the

---

1 Tweeted by Dr Jonathan Healey, Associate Professor of History at Oxford: @SocialHistoryOx.

universalization of Western liberal democracy as the final form of human government. (Fukuyama, 1989, p. 2)

Fukuyama continued this theme in his 1992 book *The End of History and the Last Man*. The irony referred to above was not lost on Derrida, who claimed that Fukuyama's book used a 'sleight-of-hand' trick of making use of empirical data whenever it seemed to suit the message, whilst appealing to an ideal when the data didn't suit; and argued thus:

> For it must be cried out, at a time when some have the audacity to neo-evangelize in the name of the ideal of a liberal democracy that has finally realized itself as the ideal of human history: never have violence, inequality, exclusion, famine, and thus economic oppression affected as many human beings in the history of the earth and of humanity. Instead of singing the advent of the ideal of liberal democracy and of the capitalist market in the euphoria of the end of history, instead of celebrating the 'end of ideologies' and the end of the great emancipatory discourses, let us never neglect this obvious macroscopic fact, made up of innumerable singular sites of suffering: no degree of progress allows one to ignore that never before, in absolute figures, have so many men, women and children been subjugated, starved or exterminated on the earth. (Derrida, 1994, p. 106)

In 2013 Milne published a book detailing much of what had occurred subsequent to Fukuyama's declaration, including the ill-fated invasion of Iraq and its consequences, entitling his book *The Revenge of History*. Bacevich (2016) argues that the US used to by and large refrain from aggressive military action, but that since the end of the Cold War, Washington's strategy changed to a more aggressive one, to try to shape the global security environment, which has in effect led to permanent war:

> Beginning in the 1990s, however, official thinking regarding the utility of force changed radically. The draft 'Defense Planning Guidance' prepared in 1991 under the aegis of Paul Wolfowitz, the U.S. undersecretary of defense for policy, hinted at the emerging mood. The mere avoidance of war no longer sufficed. Describing an international order 'shaped by the victory of the United States' over communism and in the just-concluded war against Iraq, the document identified opportunities to 'shape the future security environment in ways favourable to [the United States].'

> Shaping the future – here was an enterprise worthy of a superpower charged with fulfilling history's purpose. Lending such expectations a semblance

of plausibility was an exalted appreciation of American military might. By the early 1990s, concepts such as 'defend and deter' seemed faint-hearted, if not altogether cowardly. One army field manual from that era credited U.S. forces with the ability to achieve 'quick, decisive victory on and off the battlefield anywhere in the world and under virtually any conditions.' (Bacevich, 2016)

Bacevich (2016) urges that a new, more limited doctrine is needed, whose ultimate aims would and should be defence and deterrence.

On terrorism, whilst there have been several high-profile cases in the US and Europe over the past few years, globally it has been a tactic used by a range of groups across the world for centuries. Lenin's older brother, for example, was hanged in 1887 for his involvement in an assassination attempt on Tsar Alexander III. The First World War is sometimes blamed on the shooting of Archduke Ferdinand (although some suggest that global economic interests may have played a role). Richardson (2006) details the range of groups who have used terror, suggests that it is likely to continue to be used for the foreseeable future, and argues therefore that policy should aim at defusing and combating it on a case-by-case basis, with a proper understanding of the group being faced – their members, their motivation, their potential recruits, and so on. It is this sort of detailed work which has worked historically, rather than pursuing a 'War on Terror', in the mistaken belief that the tactic of terrorism can somehow be 'defeated', such that it would no longer be resorted to by groups in the future.[2]

> Our objective should not be the completely unattainable goal of obliterating terrorism; rather, we should pursue the more modest and attainable goal of containing terrorist recruitment and constraining resort to the tactic of terrorism. . . .

> The declaration of a global war on terrorism has been a terrible mistake and is doomed to failure. I suggest a different approach to containing terrorism, one that relies instead on an appreciation of the factors driving terrorists and is dedicated to depriving them of what they seek. We can learn from the experience of other countries in countering terrorism. We should emulate their success and avoid repeating their mistakes.

---

2 I heard a comedian suggest that since the 'War on Drugs' had led to an increase in drug crime, and the 'War on Terror' had led to an increase in terror, could we not launch a 'War on Happiness' and enjoy a concomitant increase in happiness?

Terrorism is a tactic that will continue to be employed as long as it is deemed to be effective. Technological developments will make it easier for ever smaller groups to employ weapons of ever greater lethality against us. Political, social, and economic developments will continue to produce disaffected individuals. We will never be able to prevent every attack. But we can control our reactions to those attacks. If we keep terrorist attacks in perspective and recognize that the strongest weapons in our arsenal against terrorism are precisely the hallmarks of democracy that we value, then we can indeed contain the terrorist threat. (Richardson, 2006, pp. xix, xxii)[3]

The key point here is that terror and armed conflict are indeed global challenges. But they are nothing new. Indeed, as referred to above, a terrorist act in 1914 triggered a world war, more than a century ago. Now, as then, what is needed is to handle the issue of terrorism as referred to above, and to work to build and strengthen a commitment to pursuing peaceful solutions to the world's problems, including through institutions such as the United Nations, and through education, such as the United World Colleges movement, which is committed to using education as 'a force to unite people, nations and cultures for peace and a sustainable future'.[4]

8.2 Inequality

Economic development – in particular of China but also India and other countries – has lifted hundreds of millions out of poverty. But within countries – China included – inequality has increased. This increase in inequality has been documented exhaustively by, for example, Piketty, and the sources he quotes:

> Since 1980 . . . income inequality has exploded in the United States. The upper decile's share increased from 30–35 per cent of national income in the 1970s to 45–50 per cent in the 2000s – an increase of 15 points of national income. . . .

---

3 Ironically, since writing this, Richardson has moved from Harvard and is now in the UK, as Vice-Chancellor of the University of Oxford, where the UK government's anti-terrorist 'prevent' strategy is being imposed on universities quite inappropriately.

4 Disclosure: the author is a member of the UWC Council, and Chair of the Board of Governors at UWC Atlantic College. (All royalties from this book will go to UWC Atlantic College's scholarship fund.)

The bulk of the growth of inequality came from 'the 1 per cent', whose share of national income rose from 9 per cent in the 1970s to about 20 per cent in 2000–2010 . . . 'the 5 per cent' (whose annual income ranged from $108,000 to $150,000 per household in 2010) as well as 'the 4 per cent' (whose income ranged from $150,000 to $352,000) also experienced substantial increases: the share of the former in US national income rose from 11 to 12 per cent . . . and that of the latter rose from 13 to 16 per cent. . .

In my view, there is absolutely no doubt that the increase of inequality in the United States contributed to the nation's financial instability. The reason is simple: one consequence of increasing inequality was virtual stagnation of the purchasing power of the lower and middle classes in the United States, which inevitably made it more likely that modest households would take on debt, especially since unscrupulous banks and financial intermediaries, freed from regulation and eager to earn good yields on the enormous savings injected into the system by the well-to-do, offered credit on increasingly generous terms. (Piketty, 2014, pp. 294, 296, 297)

Likewise in the UK, the top 1 per cent saw their share of income fall from 22 per cent in the Edwardian era to 5 per cent by the time Margaret Thatcher became Prime Minister in 1979 – its share has since tripled: now back up to 15 per cent and rising (Atkinson, 2015).

Some might respond, so what? Particularly if it has raised hundreds of millions out of poverty. First, there is no evidence that the increase in inequality has been a necessary condition for alleviating poverty, or even helpful; quite the contrary, the increased wealth of those at the top, created by this rise in inequality, may well have been at the expense of those in or around poverty. The question of 'so what' has been dealt with rigorously by Wilkinson and Pickett (2009) who document the harmful effects that inequality has, including on physical health, mental health, education, child well-being, social mobility, trust, and community life. They also show that inequality is positively correlated with drug abuse, imprisonment, obesity, violence, and teenage pregnancies. In addition, as Piketty argues above, this increased inequality was one of the causal factors behind the global financial crisis and recession, for which large sections of the world's population have been paying in various ways for almost ten years now. Farlow's (2013) study of the global financial crash also concludes that it was the rising income inequality in the years preceding the crisis that was the key causal factor. Tyson and Madgavkar (2016) discuss the deleterious effect on the 99 per cent of this increase in inequality – which they report all the richest countries as having suffered from, other than Sweden, which took measures to avoid the problem – and the problem that this 'great income stagnation' has on the dynamism of the economy (or rather, the resulting lack of dynamism). As Francis Bacon said in the 17th century, quoted at the start of this chapter, 'Wealth is like muck. It is not good but if it be spread'.

Hodgson (2015) shows that there have been large variations in measures of inequality across major capitalist countries, and over time, suggesting that it is certainly possible to alleviate inequality – it is not an inevitable outcome of the economic system. Or at least, it only is if we decide not to do anything about the outcome; and it is quite possible for us to do something about it.

So, if Wilkinson and Pickett are right that inequality is harmful – or at least, that the huge increase in inequality since the 1980s has been harmful, and if Hodgson is right that there is scope to tackle it (to at least get back to pre-1980s, 'Golden Age' levels), then how might we go about the task, globally? To answer this, we need to know the cause. Hodgson (2016) argues that it is not markets or competition, but rather the ownership of capital that is the root cause, and the solution is therefore a combination of wealth taxes, inheritance taxes, and employee ownership schemes.

8.3   Economic crises

The 2007–2008 global financial crisis was a good example of globalisation in action. It was, as its name suggests, global – in the sense that it impacted upon almost all the world's economies. Its causes were also global, in the sense that while the trigger may have been the sub-prime mortgages in the US, the reason it spread to be a global crisis lay in the deregulatory, free-market policies that had been pursued during the previous twenty years or so around the world, most particularly bank deregulation and the abolition of exchange controls, which permitted and enabled the speculative flow of capital globally. This crisis has been analysed now by a range of authors and studies – see for example Lysandrou (2011), Farlow (2013), Michie (2015), the Special Issue of the *Cambridge Journal of Economics* on 'The Global Financial Crisis' (July 2009) and the series of podcasts produced by Michie and Yueh at the time: www.kellogg.ox.ac.uk/discover/podcasts.

... while the nature of governments of course varied over the 1980s, 1990s and into the twenty-first century, both in the UK and internationally, in broad terms the privatisation and deregulation persisted, and the inequality of income and wealth increased, with a redistribution of income away from wages and salaries towards profits and executive remuneration. The push for continued deregulation therefore continued, being advocated by those who were benefiting materially from such policies. Thus President Clinton repealed the Glass–Steagall Act which had been introduced in response to the 1929 Wall Street Crash, to try to prevent a recurrence; this deregulation enabled high street banks to move into more speculative investment bank activities. In the UK, demutualisation led to most of the large building societies, which had been owned by their customers, being converted to shareholder-owned banks, all of which subsequently failed (such as Northern Rock) or were taken over by large shareholder-owned banks, thus reducing the corporate diversity of the financial services sector.

These developments created – or recreated, following the 1929 Wall Street Crash – the conditions for a spectacular collapse. And when it hit, the impact was global, thanks again to the deregulatory policies that had removed what buffers Keynes and others had managed to have put in place during the negotiations at Bretton Woods over the shape of the post-Second World War regulatory architecture. (Michie, 2015, pp. 97–98)

The importance of network effects is referred to below in the context of understanding and tackling climate change, and that literature is, we would argue, also key to understanding and tackling economic crises:

The US regulatory system inherited from the 1930s segmented the financial system into watertight compartments. Each segment was assigned its own classes of assets and liabilities and its own regulatory agency. Financial innovation had already undermined the system in part when deregulation in the 1990s led to the compete abandonment of the compartmentalisation of finance. Financial institutions of all sorts were basically allowed to engage in all kinds of transactions. Several things went wrong in the process. Most obviously, the regulatory structure was not reworked. The old matching of regulators to industry segments was entirely lost, leaving a confused division of labour between agencies with many overlaps and many lacunae, which the industry quickly learned to exploit. Second, as compartmentalisation was abandoned, connectivity in the financial system radically increased, a consequence entirely missed by monetary economists who only envisaged benefits from the increased opportunities to diversify that deregulation opened up. Third, the end of compartmentalisation turned out to mean also that the boundaries marking the responsibilities of the lender of last resort lost all definition. The implications of increased connectivity was eventually demonstrated for all to see when a small subsidiary *in London* of an American *insurance* company proved capable of endangering the entire US banking system, forcing the Treasury and the Federal Reserve into rescue operations mounting into the $170 billions – and still counting.

Network analysis is a novel field for economists (Goyal, 2007; Jackson, 2008). The crisis shows, I believe, that it should be given a priority in the training of economists ahead of some of the mathematical skills required by graduate programmes today. (Leijonhufvud, 2009, pp. 754–755, emphasis in the original)

As argued below, and by Foxon et al. (2013), the importance of network analysis for economics goes beyond just the issue of financial and economic crises.

8.4 Climate change

Environmental change is undoubtedly the over-riding policy issue facing humanity. It is clearly a global issue, albeit the solution will depend upon the co-operative actions of national governments.[5]

Investment in clean energy globally was $286 billion in 2015, against $130 billion for fossil fuels.[6] On some days both Germany and Portugal have managed to generate almost all their energy needs from renewables.[7] The share of electricity that the world's 20 major economies are generating from the sun and wind has risen by over 70 per cent over the past five years, from 4.6 per cent in 2010 to 8 per cent in 2015, and the figures for the UK, Italy and France are around 20 per cent, and for Germany is 36 per cent. China accounts for nearly a third of the renewables industry which globally amounts to around $330 billion.[8]

---

5 On the impact of climate change within the context of globalisation, see Grossman and Krueger (1991), O'Brien and Leichenko (2000), Tisdell (2001), Christmann and Taylor (2001) and Dietz et al. (2011).

6 Renewables 2016 Global Status Report, www.ren21.net.

7 See Peter Forbes, A guide to the latest developments as the transition to renewable energy gains speed up (review of *The Switch: How Solar, Storage and New Tech Means Cheap Power for All*, by Chris Goodall), *The Guardian*, 30 July 2016, on which this paragraph draws.

8 See Pilita Clark, Renewables jump 70 per cent in shift away from fossil fuels, *Financial Times*, 14 August 2016.

The problem with solar energy is when the sun doesn't shine, or for wind power when the wind doesn't blow. First, though, these issues are not as serious as might be commonly perceived – it is rare to have a windless day, and even when it is windless in one part of the country, elsewhere there will be wind (remembering that we are including offshore, and can share across countries); what is true is that there tends to be less wind in the summer, but there is more sun for solar at that time of year. Also, the problem is being solved in the sense that surplus electricity (generated when the sun and wind provide more than required at those times) can be used 'to create liquid hydrocarbons for fuel, plastics and other chemicals and methane to drive gas-fired power stations at times when renewables output dips' (Forbes, 2016).[9] The technologies are there to invest in, along with research and development programmes, and the fostering of further innovations (on which, see Goodall, 2016).[10] Increased research and development is needed across the whole range of technologies to make energy, transport, housing and other sectors less environmentally damaging, as well as on carbon storage and on technologies to take carbon dioxide out of the atmosphere, to try to not only halt the rise in global temperatures, but if possible to restore some of the damage done, by actually reversing to some degree at least the climate change that has been and will continue for some time to be inflicted upon the planet.

Sustainable development means 'meeting the needs of the present without compromising the ability of future generations to meet their own needs' (World Commission on Environment and Development, 1987). That meeting environmental, social and economic objectives is strongly interdependent has been widely recognised (see for example United Nations Framework Convention on Climate Change, 2010). Foxon et al. (2013, p. 188) argue that neoclassical economics is inadequate to address these challenges, because the underlying assumptions of individual rationality and marginal changes are inappropriate, citing Sraffa (1926) who had pointed to the weakness of the marginal approach for an understanding of real-world economic processes, as discussed by Marcuzzo and Rosselli (2011, pp. 224–225):

---

9 For a discussion of current advances in battery storage technologies, see for example Mockel (2016).

10 Chris Goodall, *The Switch: How Solar, Storage and New Tech Means Cheap Power for All*, Profile, 2016.

... an alert manager is constantly weighing the net product in saving of time and of annoyance to passengers, that will accrue from the aid of a second guard on an important train and considering whether it will be worth its costs. (Marshall, 1920, p. 5)

Sraffa never found this representation convincing, and made reference to it on various occasions over the years. He eventually wrote on 29 March 1963:

This suggests that his [the alert manager's] *main* task is to sack a porter here, add a coach to a train there, or shorten a platform elsewhere. The idea is that the process of change can be reduced to a continuous process, like shortening platforms. 'A penny is the basis of a million', and so a process of shortening, adding, sacking in detail is the route from one position to another. In Marshall's view the 'alert Dr. B' never needs to take a bird's eye view of his enterprise.

Foxon et al. (2013, p. 188) report that Marcuzzo and Rosselli go on to describe Sraffa's more fundamental objections to marginalism:

[N]ot just for its lack of realism but also for the logical impossibility of attributing effects to marginal additions of factors, when what one is really comparing is two states of the world and the difference between them is not due simply to the additional factors, but to the fact that all factors may be relating and operating differently in the second regime. But the above description of the railway manager is a nice illustration of the need to go beyond marginalism to take a 'bird's eye view', especially since this broader vision is absolutely vital to seeing the bigger picture as regards environmental sustainability and to envisioning the sort of policy measures that will be needed to achieve it.

Instead, Foxon et al. (2013) argue for a change in economic policy and approach, to tackle climate change through altering our current consumption patterns and our production technologies, and also argue that to bring about such changes, a different sort of economic analysis is needed than the mainstream 'marginalism' – one that can see the bigger picture, of how societies and economies do actually develop, and that recognises the importance of institutions, history, and culture. In addition, though, to drawing on evolutionary and institutional economics, they point to complexity theory and complexity economics as representing an important and useful research programme for the sort of intellectual and policy work that the current environmental challenges call for. The key insights from complex systems thinking are that:

[E]conomies are open, *dynamic* systems, not in equilibrium, and are made up of diverse *agents* who lack perfect foresight, but who are able to learn and adapt over time. These agents interact through various social *networks* and macro patterns *emerge* from these micro behaviours and interactions. *Evolutionary* processes create novelty and growing order and complexity over time. . . .

The dynamic, systemic nature of long-term industrial change highlights the fact that learning, scale, adaptation and network effects can give rise to increasing returns or positive feedbacks in the adoption of new technologies and institutions, so that the more they are adopted, the more likely they are to be further adopted. (Foxon et al., 2013, p. 202, emphasis in the original)[11]

The key policy conclusions and implications are that a whole *range* of measures should be pursued: economic incentives on their own are insufficient. The sorts of measures required are set out, analysed and discussed by the various contributors to Dietz et al. (2011), including the need to deploy renewable energy technologies, carbon capture and storage technology; to improve energy efficiency at home and in business; to reduce deforestation; to change consumption patterns and behaviours; and to pursue research and development, and technological innovation, to assist the above processes. Reforming agriculture is also vital: 25 per cent of greenhouse gas emissions currently are being caused by agriculture and changes in land use. Reducing these emission levels are particularly challenging given that more than a billion people in the world today are undernourished, and it is estimated that agricultural production will need to rise by at least 50 per cent by the year 2050 to feed the expected population of nine billion, and with climate change already undermining crop yields through droughts, floods, and a generally more erratic climate (see Voegele and Roome, 2016). Thus, farmers need to be assisted to grow more, be more resilient to climate change, and reduce greenhouse gas emissions from livestock, crops, and land use change – including in parts of the world such as Africa where farming is already being undermined by climate change. The World Bank is involved in 'climate-smart' agricultural projects that help to deliver such objectives, including by using climate-smart crop varieties. When the plans to create the World Bank were being formulated at Bretton Woods, it was in the context of the need for the world

---

11 For further discussion of complexity theory, which also argues that it, combined with evolutionary theory, can and should replace mainstream neoclassical economics as a way of analysing the economy, see Wilson (2016).

economy to recover from world war, and then to enable economies to develop, including those emerging from colonialism, with all that that entailed in terms of economic legacy. Today's needs are different, with the overarching requirement being sustainable development to tackle climate change. That needs to be made the central objective and aim of the World Bank for the forthcoming era of global development – delivering a green new deal, globally.[12]

Townsend (2016, 2017) gives an excellent outline of 'the circular economy', arguing for a new business model to reduce built-in obsolescence, encourage repair and re-use, and pursue other such avenues to act on both consumption and production to reduce damage to the environment. Governments need to do more to prevent built-in obsolescence and incentivise and reward repair and re-use. Sweden, for example, is to cut VAT on repairs to bicycles, clothes and shoes from 25 per cent to 12 per cent, and allow costs of repairing other items to be reclaimed from income tax.

8.5   Conclusion

The above challenges are 'global' issues in every sense. It is the future of the planet at risk. And we need all governments, global institutions, regional and local governments, and other institutions, to be acting in concert. Before proceeding to a discussion of what sort of policy measures and approaches might be appropriate and effective in this regard, in Chapter 10, we turn first to one further global issue, namely taxation.

---

12 For a detailed analysis of the key issues around globalisation and agriculture, see the various contributors to Robinson and Carson (2015).

9 Tax competition, avoidance and evasion and unproductive capital

[The Simpsons: In the Cayman Islands, a representative of the Cayman Islands Offshore Holding Corporation has just received a phone call, inquiring about Krusty the Clown's account.]
Representative: I'm sorry. I cannot divulge information about that customer's secret, illegal account.
[The representative hangs up the phone, then does a double take as he realizes what he just did.]
Representative: Oh, crap, I shouldn't have said he was a customer. Oh, crap, I shouldn't have said it was a secret. Oh, crap! I certainly shouldn't have said it was illegal! [sighs resignedly] Oh, it's too hot today.

It has long been recognised that corporations seek to avoid or even evade taxation, as do wealthy individuals. On definitions: 'tax avoidance' is legal, utilising arrangements that are within the law to minimise tax liability; 'tax evasion' is illegal – failing to pay taxes without any legal justification for having so failed. However, we would suggest that deliberate and wilful tax avoidance should also be made illegal – that is, where the activity is clearly seeking to circumvent what Parliament (or the government) is seeking to achieve with their tax laws. Such wilful circumvention should become akin to perverting the course of justice. And all those involved in the activity should be liable – not just the person or company avoiding tax, but also the bankers, accountants, lawyers and other advisors who assist with the process – who conspire to pervert the aims and intentions of the tax system and its arrangements.

One mechanism for tax evasion by companies is 'transfer pricing'. For example, Chapter 2 referred to General Motors' decision to establish a factory in Germany in the 1930s to help supply the Nazi army.[1] Suppose

---

1 In the interests of balance, it should be pointed out that Ford did likewise, and that Hitler had a picture of Henry Ford hanging in his office, being a great admirer of Henry Ford's anti-Semitic views.

that this factory imported components from its US plant. The relative profitability of the US and German operations would depend on how much the company decides to charge itself for the components; so, this can be manipulated to report higher profits in the jurisdiction with the lower corporate profit rate. Currently, this is one of the practices that the European Commission is investigating in relation to Apple's failure to pay proper levels of tax.

Two major categories of problems that have been identified with such behaviour – tax avoidance and tax evasion – are first the political and ethical problems, and second the economic and fiscal ones. On the first category, politically it cannot be helpful for it to be known that some are deliberately breaking the law in order to evade taxes, thus leaving it for others to have to contribute more, to make up the shortfall; and similarly for tax avoidance. Such knowledge – and the fact that the political establishment appears to be permitting such behaviours – will have a corrosive effect on the ethical culture of society.

On the second category, economically, the taxation is required to fund government expenditures, so any shortfall caused by tax avoidance and evasion will cause fiscal difficulties. Either the lower revenues are accepted, with borrowing being higher than planned, or spending programmes being cut. Or alternatively, the shortfall would need to be made up by imposing higher taxation on those who do pay their taxes.

To these long-recognised issues, I would add an additional one which is in my view of significant and growing importance: namely, that tax avoidance and evasion risks making capital *unproductive*, by withdrawing it from the productive system. Significantly, I would argue, this risk has become an increasing problem over recent years, as the extent of tax avoidance and evasion globally has grown. This growth has been fuelled by the 'capitalism unleashed' era of globalisation which has created great opportunities, most starkly with the restoration of capitalism in the former Soviet Union; the abolition of capital controls which has permitted a global free-for-all in terms of moving funds across borders; deregulation which tempted many banks into these more speculative and even illegal areas of activity (as documented in the case of Deutsche Bank above); increased inequality which has boosted the wealth of the already very wealthy, thus increasing their incentive to hide these fortunes; and austerity measures which have reduced the capacity of revenue authorities to collect revenues.

This growing problem – of an increasing proportion of the world's capital becoming unproductive – is, I would argue, fuelled by three major developments. First, the abolition of capital controls in the 'capitalism unleashed' variety of globalisation has led to a lower proportion of capital going on productive uses, such as investing in factories and other productive facilities, and a growing proportion going on speculation. Second, a growing proportion of capital is being hidden in accounts to avoid or evade taxation, and in most cases this means that such capital will not be put to productive use. It is either left idle, or it is used for other hidden activities, such as the drugs, arms, and human trafficking trades. Third, the growth in inequality has shifted wealth from the mass of the population – who would generally spend all they receive on goods and services, thus generating demand and jobs – to the wealthiest 1 per cent, and even more so the wealthiest 0.1 per cent, who are more likely to hoard much of their income and wealth, in effect withdrawing it from the system. (What they do spend will include buying private jets and the like, which are often environmentally damaging, but that is a separate point, albeit another negative one.)

In addition to these problems of tax avoidance and evasion, is that of 'tax competition' – the race to the bottom where some countries offer lower tax rates in order to try to attract tax-paying companies or individuals from other countries. This chapter discusses these problems in turn, concluding that the new threat of capital becoming unproductive is becoming a serious drain on the world's productive capacity; and that the extent of this damage is not only serious and growing, but also unpredictable, thus adding a further element of uncertainty, risk and instability to the global economy. Before turning to these problems, we first discuss proposals for additional taxes – wealth taxes, and a transactions tax on international financial speculation.

9.1   Wealth taxes and a transactions' tax

Many countries have wealth taxes in addition to income tax, inheritance tax, consumption taxes, corporate taxes, and so on. The logic of having wealth taxes has become stronger over the past few years and decades as inequalities in wealth have ballooned globally. Such taxes not only provide additional revenues for governments to utilise, but also help in reducing the huge increases in wealth inequalities we have witnessed in practically every country in the world over the past few years and decades. Piketty, in his study of the growth in the inequality of income and wealth across the world, concludes that wealth taxes could and should play an important part of tackling this growing problem.

The other tax that is required, internationally, is on international speculation. This has been advocated for decades, and was referred to initially as the 'Tobin Tax' after James Tobin, the Nobel Prize winning economist who advocated it. More recently it has been referred to as a 'Robin Hood' tax, as it would take from the rich, and could be used for the benefit of the poor, funding schemes globally to promote sustainable development, for example. The idea of the Tobin Tax is set out and analysed in detail by, for example, the various contributors to ul Haq et al. (1996). Arestis and Sawyer (2013) examine the potential of a large number of such financial transaction taxes, and conclude that:

> A range of financial transaction taxes would be a route to addressing the relative undertaxing of the financial sector and its activities. Such taxes can be designed in a way that stimulates the economy, depending on how the taxes are structured, how the overall tax revenue is affected, and the uses to which the funds raised by financial transactions are put. (Arestis and Sawyer, 2013, p. 115)[2]

A key point to grasp is that while economists generally present taxes as distorting the market, the point of this tax is to do precisely that – because the operation of 'the market' is so hugely damaging to the global economy and hence to people's well-being across the world. The architect, economist James Tobin, described the point as to put some 'sand in the wheels' of such markets – to slow them down or deter them.

9.2   Globalisation, taxation and the welfare state

On the difficulty of taxing mobile capital, Swank (1998) reports that there is little evidence of such a process actually occurring. Indeed, the evidence suggests that the size of the state budget (and the amount of taxation raised by governments) is positively correlated with the degree of economic openness, rather than negatively correlated (which might be expected if an increased degree of economic openness made

---

2 See also Arestis and Sawyer (1999).

it more difficult to extract taxation from footloose capital and people – or at least increased their options for avoiding or evading tax). Dani Rodrik, on the basis of a quantitative study of state expenditures in one hundred countries, which showed a general connection between economic openness and the size of the state budget, suggests that this may indeed be causal, with increased economic openness creating risks and potential instability for the economy, hence requiring increased government involvement to mitigate those risks, and to work to offset any such resulting instability:

> Contrary to what most economists would expect, the scope of government has been larger, not smaller, in economies taking greater advantage of world markets. Indeed, governments have expanded faster in the most open economies. The evidence considered here suggests strongly that the reasons have to do with the risks of being exposed to shocks of external origin. Openness exerts the strongest influence on government consumption in economies which are subject to the greatest amounts of terms-of-trade risk. Governments appear to have sought to mitigate the exposure to external risk by increasing the share of domestic output which they consume. Of course, on *a priori* grounds, it is not altogether clear that a higher share of government consumption can stabilise incomes. But I have provided some evidence that the government sector can indeed be considered as the 'safe' sector – in the empirically relevant sense – for the vast majority of countries. (Rodrik, 1996, p. 26)

Iversen and Cusack (2000) argue that deindustrialisation is a cause of welfare spending. However, this begs the question of what has caused the deindustrialisation, and clearly the form of free-market globalisation, with off-shoring, has played a part. For developing countries with a high proportion of low-skilled workers, Rudra (2002) finds that globalisation has indeed resulted in lower welfare spending.[3] Korpi and Palme (2003) argue that the main cause of welfare state 'regress' has been austerity – and note that this was before the post-2009 Great Recession austerity measures. Brady, Beckfield and Seeleib-Kaiser (2005) also see political and economic factors having a greater impact on welfare states than globalisation. And Rieger and Leibfried (1998, pp. 380–381) argue that the greatest impact of globalisation on welfare states is to make the welfare state orient itself increasingly to the status quo:

---

3 For a discussion of the effects that globalisation has had on the balance of political power in Latin America, impacting upon governments' fiscal commitments to social security, health, and education, see Kaufman and Segura-Ubiergo (2001).

[W]ith growing external pressures from globalisation, the capacity to adapt national social policy shrinks. The radical change in US welfare policy in 1996 – the discontinuation of a federal guarantee of a right to welfare, the introduction of time limits for income transfers, the devolution of welfare to the states – indicates how a relatively low level of globalisation pressure goes hand in hand with a broad capacity for massive change, while in Western Europe and Germany a high level of external pressure seems almost to prohibit any change in the social policy status quo.

Clearly there are various multi-directional links between globalisation, other political and economic factors, deindustrialisation, and welfare state and other government spending (and corresponding levels of taxation).[4] Free-market policies have promoted globalisation, exacerbated deindustrialisation, sought to cut back the welfare state, and reduced taxation. Globalisation, in turn, has exacerbated deindustrialisation and both increased the need for a strong welfare state at the same time as undermining the tax-raising capacity of governments to deliver on this increased need; it is to this tax-raising capacity that we now turn.

9.3   Tax competition

Countries from Panama to the Republic of Ireland have offered low – or no – tax rates to companies in the hope of attracting them to move there. Some companies have indeed taken advantage of these opportunities in order to reduce the amount they pay in tax. Thus, for example, Google's global head of tax, Tom Hutchinson, told the UK Parliament's public accounts committee in February 2016 that the company's worldwide tax rate over the previous five years averaged around 19 per cent. This compares to the UK rate of corporation tax over those years averaging over 23 per cent, and in the US 35 per cent plus local state taxes. The reason for Google's relatively low rate of tax payments include the fact that they register much of their business in Ireland, with 18 billion euros worth of international sales routed through Dublin, including £5 billion worth of UK sales. One aspect of such arrangements is that it is not clear how much the home country benefits from attracting such company registrations. Thus, in July 2016

---

4 Indeed, Rieger and Leibfried (1998) see the welfare state as actually facilitating globalisation, since without the welfare state, people would not put up with the negative consequences of globalisation, and hence would not permit its promotion to the extent that they have done.

the Irish Central Statistics Office reported their economy as having grown in 2015 in real terms by 26.3 per cent. This clearly bears no relation to what was actually happening in the economy, which would have grown by less than a quarter of that figure. Rather, such figures represent the effects of companies moving their registrations in and out of that country, and varying the amount of business that they report as having flowed through the part of their company registered there. Such an approach is clearly unhelpful to countries taken together – and even for the 'beneficiaries', it can be potentially destabilising.[5]

Avi-Yonah (2000) examines the increased use of tax incentives as weapons in the international competition to attract investment. This most obviously takes the form of setting tax at rates lower than pertain in other countries, with the aim of getting companies and individuals to migrate to the lower-tax jurisdiction. Avi-Yonah (2000) suggests tackling such behaviour through a coordinated imposition of withholding taxes on international portfolio investment, with the aim of ensuring that all income may be taxed in the investor's home jurisdiction, and that multinational companies be taxed in the jurisdictions where their goods and services are consumed.[6]

At the time of writing (March 2017), the European Commission is seeking to force Google to pay billions of dollars' worth of taxes to the Irish government, on the basis that the Irish government had no right to allow the company to avoid paying the tax that other companies in Ireland were liable for. The Irish government object to having to collect this tax. It does seem perverse to force a government to accept money it doesn't wish to collect. Better surely for such funds to be collected by a global authority, to help fund the much-needed global Green New Deal.

9.4   Tax avoidance and evasion

In addition to the above problem of tax competition, Avi-Yonah (2000) argues that:

---

5 See for example Vincent Boland, 'Multinationals Obscure Real State of Ireland's Economy', *Financial Times*, 15 August 2016.

6 For an interesting and useful collection of articles on the problems and prospect for taxation in the developing world, see the April 2016 special issue of the *Review of International Political Economy*, Volume 23, Number 2.

... the establishment of tax havens allows large amounts of capital to go untaxed, depriving both developed and developing countries of revenue and forcing them to rely on forms of taxation less progressive than the income tax.

There has been much international action seeking to tackle these problems – of tax competition, as well as tax avoidance and evasion – including from the OECD. UK governments have often claimed to be supportive, but there are doubts as to how seriously UK governments have ever really pursued such action, with some suspicion that they have actually sought to block and undermine such efforts.[7]

The issue hit the headlines globally in April 2016 with the leak of more than 11.5 million documents from the Panama-based law firm Mossack Fonseca – the so-called 'Panama Papers', which detailed financial information from offshore accounts and tax evasion by the rich and powerful, revealing amongst other things $2 billion flowing from Russian banks to offshore companies; a secret British Virgin Islands firm owned by Iceland's Prime Minister Sigmundur Davio Gunnlaugsson, who resigned after 10,000 of the country's 330,000 population protested outside Parliament in Reykjavik, calling for him to quit; the investment fund company owned by David Cameron's late father had not paid any UK tax on its profits in all its 30 years of trading (Cameron resigned as prime minister later that year, but this was because of having called and lost a referendum on the UK's membership of the European Union, rather than in response to this revelation from the Panama Papers); companies owned by a Zimbabwean arms dealer and a mining tycoon, despite these being blacklisted by the EU; Mossack Fonseca acted for an Iranian oil company which was blacklisted in the US; details of many offshore companies owned by over 800 suspected tax evaders being pursued by Australian's tax office; and China and Hong Kong were Mossack Fonseca's biggest sources of business, with Chinese clients linked to 40,000 companies. The Panama Papers cover a period from 1977 to December 2015; in addition to those listed above, other dealings include companies involving Pakistan, Syria, and Argentina.

---

7 UK Prime Minister David Cameron personally lobbied against EU plans to name the owners of offshore trusts; this was before it was discovered that he and his wife had been owners of his late father's offshore trust, referred to below, which the Panama Papers revealed had paid no UK tax whatsoever over its 30 years of operations.

Panama's President Varela created a seven-member international panel to help improve transparency in the country's offshore financial industry, including Nobel Prize winning economist Joseph Stiglitz and Swiss anti-corruption expert Mark Pieth, a criminal law professor at Basel University. In August 2016 both Stiglitz and Pieth resigned from the panel in protest at the failure to agree to make public the panel's findings. As I tweeted at the time, 'What are the chances? Investigation of cover-up is being covered up.'

In October 2015, the G20 pledged to pursue an unprecedented international collaboration on tax reform, following a two-year programme under the auspices of the Organisation for Economic Co-operation and Development (OECD), aiming to wipe out much of the world's tax avoidance industry. The OECD released estimates suggesting that large global businesses were avoiding between 4 per cent and 10 per cent of their tax liabilities (£65 billion to £160 billion a year) – although this was said to be a conservative estimate, meaning it is probably higher. The reform programme is backed by sixty countries, representing more than 90 per cent of the world's economy. However, many of the recommendations are voluntary, leaving it to individual countries to decide whether or not to implement them. It is unlikely that this major international problem will be solved until and unless binding rules are introduced.[8]

9.5   Capital becoming unproductive and criminal

According to Henry (2016a), the Panama Papers revelations 'are small when compared to the actual size of global financial crime':

> Panama, after all, is only one of more than 90 financial secrecy jurisdictions around the world today, compared with just a dozen or so in the early 1970s. Together, as of 2015, they hold at least $24 trillion to $36 trillion in anonymous private financial wealth, most of which belong to the top 0.1 per cent of the planet's wealthiest. . . .

> According to our estimates, the global stock of unrecorded private financial net assets – including currency, bank deposits, stocks and bonds, and other tradable securities – invested in or through offshore havens already totalled $21 trillion to $32 trillion by the end of 2010, about 10–15 per cent of global

---

8 See for example Simon Bowers, 'OECD hopes tax reforms will end era of aggressive avoidance', *The Guardian*, 5 October 2015.

financial wealth. And this 'missing' wealth stock has continued to grow since then. Indeed, from 2004 to 2015, right through the financial crisis, it grew at a nominal annual average rate of nearly 16 per cent a year. As of 2015, this 'missing' stock of offshore private financial wealth was worth at least $24 trillion to $36 trillion.

In addition, the value of non-financial net cross-border wealth – real estate, gold and other precious metals, precious gems, art, rare books, cars, religious icons, photos, other collectibles, yachts, ships, submarines, private jets, real estate, farms, mines, forests, and oil fields – that is owned through anonymous haven companies, trusts, foundations, and private vaults – is now worth at least another $5 trillion to $10 trillion.

It is difficult for such funds, which are illegally avoiding the tax authorities, to be put to legitimate, productive use, precisely because they must remain hidden.[9] This capital is thus rendered unproductive, no longer available to invest in productive activities. Such funds either lie dormant, or if they are put to use then it has to be in other hidden activities, such as arms or drug trafficking. This withdrawal of capital from the global economy represents a huge loss of funding for investment, enterprise, and productive activity. Ending tax avoidance and evasion is not only the right thing to do on moral, ethical and legal grounds, and hence important for the good of society; and not only would the tax revenue then be available for funding both social and productive infrastructure and activities – health and education, and also transport and communications; but the return of these vast quantities of capital to the real economy could provide a significantly positive boost to the world economy and for global development.

9.6   How significant is tax evasion?

A 2015 report from two strategists in the research department of Deutsche Bank in London, Oliver Harvey and Robin Winkler, 'Dark matter' described 'the vast unrecorded transfer of money among nations' (Caesar, 2016):

---

9 The Panama Papers show that some companies set up in tax havens may have been used for money laundering, and for arms and drugs deals, as well as for tax evasion. The panel member Pieth, referred to above, said 'I have had a close look at the so called Panama Papers and I must admit that, even as an expert on economic and organised crime, I was amazed to see so much of what we talk about in theory was confirmed in practice.'

The report's conclusions confirmed long-held suspicions. In any national economy, the authors explained, there are capital flows that do not appear on what is called 'the balance of payments'. Errors and accidental omissions should be random, and therefore reveal no pattern. The authors found that in the United Kingdom the pattern was anything but random. Britain had 'large positive net errors' that suggested significant 'unrecorded capital out-flows'. Analyzing data from other countries, Harvey and Winkler deduced where the vast majority of unrecorded capital flowing into the U.K. was coming from. Since 2010, they wrote, about a billion and a half dollars had arrived, unrecorded, in London *every month*; 'a good chunk' of it was from Russia. (Caesar, 2016)

According to a separate internal Deutsche Bank report, around ten billion US dollars were transferred out of Russia between 2011 and 2015 through a single money-laundering scheme, just from Deutsche Bank's Moscow office (Caesar, 2016). Caesar (2016) reports that such transfers have had a noticeable effect on London property prices, and currency movements.[10] (In September 2016 Deutsche Bank was fined $14 billion by the US Department of Justice for mis-selling mortgage bonds from 2005 to 2007.)

The 500 largest US companies were estimated to be holding more than $2.1 trillion in 2014 in accumulated profits overseas to avoid US taxes (Richter, 2015). According to Richard Lane, an analyst at Moody's, the figure at the end of 2015 was $1.2 trillion for companies outside the financial sector (as reported by Fleming and Jopson, 2016).

9.7   Policy – preventing tax avoidance and evasion and putting capital to work

UK Treasury and tax officials are, at the time of writing, planning to introduce new measures to counter tax avoidance, by targeting the accountants, lawyers and other advisors who design and recommend the tax avoidance schemes, including the big accounting firms. Those found to be involved in such schemes would be fined, up to the full

---

10 'The impact of this capital flight is felt at both ends of its journey. Research published last year by Deutsche Bank's own analysis suggested that unrecorded capital inflows from Russia into the U.K. correlated strongly with increases in U.K. house prices and, to a lesser extent, with a strengthen-ing of the pound sterling. Capital flight also has weakened Russia's tax base and its currency' (Caesar, 2016).

amount of the tax avoided.[11] It is estimated that of the tax currently foregone, that such a policy could recoup amounts to between £3 billion and £9 billion a year in the UK (the wide range of the estimated value reflecting of course its illegal and hidden nature). The increased revenues might be made up from a combination of increased tax payments, alongside fines on those who continue to seek to avoid tax.[12]

The proposals in the UK Treasury document are that it is only where schemes are defeated in the courts by HM Revenue and Customs that the fines would become payable. Currently the tax avoiders themselves face financial costs if defeated in court, but those who advise and facilitate the avoidance bear little risk. It is this which would change. Opening the 12-week consultation, the financial secretary to the Treasury, Jane Ellison, said 'People who peddle tax avoidance schemes deny the country vital tax revenue and this government is determined to make sure they pay.' In Australia, promoters of tax avoidance schemes have to receive permission from the tax office before implementing them. That seems an obvious and unobjectionable process.

9.8   Conclusion: capital isn't working

Many parts of the world economy have suffered almost a decade of stagnation since the 2007–2008 global financial crisis. Some fear a new era of such stagnation. Note that such stagnation will not necessarily be useful in tackling climate change. That requires large-scale investment in renewable energy technologies, environmentally friendly farming, housing, and transport schemes, and so on. A stagnant economy is not the most promising base from which to develop such programmes. A 'low growth' or even 'no growth' strategy to tackle climate change is much better developed where the economy is productive, and it can be a conscious and deliberate decision to collectively take more leisure time, reduce the average working week, and change consumption patterns along more sustainable lines. Instead, the current stagnationist tendency is being caused by capital being withdrawn from the productive system by a combination of a free-for-all to use capital for

---

11 Plans published by the UK Treasury in a consultation document released on 17 August 2016.

12 A leading critic of tax avoidance, Professor of Accounting Prem Sikka, warns both that the proposals are too weak, in cracking down only on schemes that are deemed unlawful in court rather than on all advice on avoidance, and also that the UK government is not providing the judicial capacity to implement the proposals.

speculation rather than production; tax avoidance and evasion withdrawing vast quantities of wealth from the productive system, to be either hoarded, or used for criminal activities such as the drugs trade; and increased inequality leading to a super-rich elite who have more wealth than they can productively use. Each of these factors – lack of capital controls, tax evasion, and increased inequality – has various other deleterious effects on society. But they also combine to create a perfect storm of capital withdrawal from productive use.

10 Policy implications for governments and political parties

Microeconomists are people who are wrong about specific things, whereas macroeconomists are wrong about things in general.

(Yoram Bauman, 2007)[1]

National economies, international financial markets, and businesses are all complex, dynamic, non-linear systems, about which it is almost impossible to make specific predictions (Kay, 2009). From this, Thompson (2011, p. 51) argues that 'if financial crises are fundamentally "irrational" – driven by "excessive exuberances", "animal spirits", "bandwagon effects", "bubbles", Ponzi schemes, exotic calculative technologies, and the like – then we should prepare ourselves in quite a different manner than so far for the next crisis – because there will be one.' In terms of how we should prepare ourselves, his conclusion is two-fold. First, he argues that despite globalisation, the financial system is still very different from country to country, and the super-national blocks such as NAFTA and the EU play an important role, so rather than looking for global top-down solutions, we should be developing policies appropriate for each country and for each 'regional block', in a bottom-up approach. Second, he argues that the international financial system is almost by definition 'irrational', and not therefore fully amenable to systemic and calculative responses. What is needed therefore:

[I]s to organise a highly flexible regulatory regime of 'distributed preparedness for resilience', one that does not presume a single centre from which a new elaborate global regulatory regime emanates (Collier and Lakoff, 2008). . . .

And whilst it will be difficult for those states that have socialized large sections of their financial systems to return these to private ownership

---

1 Yoram Bauman, Mankiw's Ten Principles of Economics, Translated, AAAS humor session, 16 February 2007, www.standupeconomist.com.

quickly, this is not necessarily a priority. It may be that a newly formulated regulatory regime will require a continued presence of public ownership of significant parts of the financial system, if nothing else because of the analysis above indicating the difficulty of kick-starting the credit/money production process without it. And this may be the only effective way to deal with the continued dispersed character of the international financial system and to prepare for the resilience necessary to deal with new unexpected eruptions as they happen, because these will happen whatever is done. (Thompson, 2011, pp. 53-54)

In terms of policy recommendations, this chimes strongly with several themes that have emerged throughout this book, including first, the importance of realising that the economic system is not a self-righting equilibrium system. Rather, it is prone to instability, with the danger of becoming stuck in recession (Keynes, 1936), and of cumulative causation leading to increased divergence in performance between leading and lagging sectors, regions, and economies. Second, the importance of national economic policy, notwithstanding the importance of international economic policy. Third, the importance of appreciating that individuals and companies operate in and are influenced by networks, rather than making decisions individually unaffected by others (Ormerod, 2016). Fourth, the importance of creating and enhancing regional resilience in order to strengthen the economic position of communities, and even of whole countries (Christopherson et al., 2008). And fifth, the importance of recognising the usefulness of public and mutual ownership, alongside the usefulness of private ownership.

One implication of globalisation – or at least the form that has been pursued with capitalism unleashed – is that national governments are constrained in the policy action they can take. This was demonstrated when Greece elected an anti-austerity Syriza[2] Government in 2015, with their Finance Minister Yanis Varoufakis being told, during a meeting with EU officials, that policy could not be changed, as commitments had been made. Sure enough, the European Union and the International Monetary Fund refused to compromise on the 2010 bailout conditions, against which Syriza had been elected. Syriza is now implementing those policies. So, clearly, there are constraints, and political parties need to be mindful of these constraints, and how they

---

2 Syriza is an acronym for Coalition of the Radical Left.

might be avoided, circumvented or otherwise tackled, when drawing up their political programmes, and making commitments.

A few caveats should be made, however. The first is that the Syriza government was particularly constrained, as it was heavily in debt to foreign creditors – perhaps the most difficult situation to be in. Nevertheless, there were other options. They could have defaulted, or left the euro, or both. Ironically, the reason the international institutions were quite so harsh was not because they thought the Greek electorate was undeserving or unreasonable, nor that the creditors couldn't afford – in economic terms – to allow a bit of flexibility. On the contrary, many recognised that the Greek electorate had a point, and that the austerity measures would leave the Greek economy even less able to pay – a bit like the German economy after the First World War when Britain insisted that the allies impose unrealistically harsh reparation payments, which Keynes warned would be both damaging and counterproductive. And a different deal would have been perfectly affordable to the creditors. The real problem was the ideological commitment that the creditors had to the single-currency euro project, which they had implemented in the face of warnings that it was ill-conceived and was doomed to create rather than solve problems. So the model was stuck to rigidly because of an obsession with the model, rather than because of the rights or wrongs of the Greek electorate's case.

The other major caveat is one being made throughout this book, that although today everything seems to be changing fast, and appears vastly different to previously, this much has generally been the case historically. So in that sense nothing has changed. There is no doubt that as part of the capitalism unleashed programme, powers have been deliberately passed from governments to the corporate sector, so that elected governments have been made weaker – by the deliberate actions of those elected governments. But it's not a new phenomenon, just a matter of degree. Thus, when in the 19th century the Chinese wished to pursue policies which they felt were in the interests of their country, they were met with British gunboats and the opium wars, and ended up having to give way (and to give away Hong Kong – until Chris Patten returned it). When Spain elected a left government in 1936 it faced a fascist challenge from General Franco, supported by Nazi Germany and Mussolini's Italy, whilst Britain stood on the side-lines claiming that no-one was intervening – as the 1936–1939 Spanish Civil War led to the elected government being replaced by a Fascist one. (Whilst there were no iPhones to film the German blitzkrieg, Picasso did at least depict the scenes from Guernica subsequently.) When Chile elected a left government in 1970, Western media reported it was safe from the military, as Chile had the longest history of parliamentary democracy in South America. The US put paid to that with the 1973 coup. And so on. So, what are the options for political commitments being made by parties in national governments, in this era of globalisation?

These might usefully be divided into two categories: first, policies such as on employment, housing, education, health, local government services, and so forth, for which the nature of globalisation today as opposed to ten, fifty or a hundred years ago does not necessarily impact or constrain greatly. There is a question about capacity to raise tax revenues, and hence possibly how generous or ambitious such policies can afford to be, but with that caveat, the bulk of what the electorate are concerned with, will not necessarily be greatly constrained by today's degree and nature of globalisation.

Second are those policies which may be constrained significantly by today's globalisation. This includes monetary and exchange rate policy, where the free movement of capital makes it more difficult for governments to pursue their desired outcomes, and taxation, given that companies and individuals may be more mobile than before, and thus able thereby to avoid paying taxes.

Before discussing these, we should focus on one overarching area which really is a matter of life or death for the human race, and – in part for that reason – actually cuts across and has to be included in each of the above three areas, namely climate change. Following this discussion, some potential policy ideas are brought together at the end of the chapter, not to be prescriptive, but rather to give a flavour of the sort of policy package that might be relevant for governments within today's globalisation environment.

10.1   Climate change and a Green New Deal

The need to halt – and if possible reverse – climate change must be the over-riding policy priority. What is needed – in both 'macro' and 'micro' terms – is a 'Green New Deal'. The term is an echo of President Roosevelt's New Deal in 1930s America, to create jobs during the

Great Depression. The aim today has to be to reduce carbon emissions. At a macro level this requires government legislating, regulating, and investing in green technologies and in an environmentally sustainable productive and social infrastructure (energy, transport, housing, farming, health, education, and so on). At a micro level it requires changes in business practices and management decision-making, as well as in consumer behaviour. The case for a Green New Deal has been made by numerous authors and organisations, including the New Economics Foundation (2008) and the UN Environment Programme (2008), as discussed by, for example, Dietz et al. (2011), Foxon et al. (2013), Mazzucato (2013) and Harcourt (2014).

One of the major contributors to the carbon emissions that are doing so much damage to the environment is the energy sector. A starting point must therefore be to reduce the demand for energy. There is undoubtedly huge scope for this in all countries, through investing in both domestic and industrial energy efficiency. It is estimated that in the UK, an investment of less than £1 billion a year in domestic and industrial energy efficiency could halve energy demand by 2050. This should be the absolute top priority, in policy terms, for tackling climate change: *investing in domestic and industrial energy efficiency to reduce the demand for energy.*

That leaves the question of how to generate the energy that is still required. Clearly the aim needs to be to provide as great a share of this from renewables, and as small a proportion as possible from coal and oil. One controversial area is how nuclear energy should be regarded on environmental grounds, given that it scores well in terms of greenhouse gas emissions, but poses environmental hazards both when operating, in the event of accidents, and in the longer term during and subsequent to decommissioning. In the UK, a new nuclear power station was commissioned in 2016 at Hinkley Point, with estimated building costs of £18 billion plus subsequent running subsidies of £30 billion, totalling £48 billion, which if history is anything to go by will almost certainly over-run, to more than £50 billion, possibly well over. An alternative would have been to have devoted that £50 billion to a programme of renewable energy. The Dogger Bank Wind Farm has a range of ambitions in terms of capacity and cost, with the more ambitious providing greater capacity than the nuclear power plant, yet at less cost. Interconnection with Norway, Denmark and France according to fluctuating demand levels would be a nice example of positive globalisation – or at least, international co-operation. This would leave the remainder of the £50 billion to go towards other renewable projects – *investing in solar, hydroelectric, wave, and tidal power.*

Another major contributor to carbon emissions is air travel and transport. Aeroplane manufacturers are already making more fuel-efficient planes, with the Boeing 787 and Airbus A350 more fuel-efficient than the models they replaced, and the International Civil Aviation Organization is developing regulation to cut the carbon emissions from commercial aircraft. These developments need to be encouraged and pushed further, and with measures to reduce the number of flights made, including through sourcing materials and components locally, rather than flying them round the world, *cutting transport emissions through regulation, innovation, and localisation.*

In addition to the above reference to investing in domestic energy efficiency, there is the far more wide-ranging and ambitious goal of *altering consumer behaviour.* Jackson (2011) argues that government action to date has tended to be limited to either informational campaigns, or taxation policies, and that the success of both strands is limited by the consumption-driven nature of our societies, in which governments are complicit, and this more fundamental issue needs to be addressed. Similarly, Whitmarsh (2011) argues that public policy needs to *foster public engagement* in environmental issues and low-carbon lifestyles, rather than just treat the public as consumers. In the meantime, it is encouraging that introducing a small charge (five pence) for single-use plastic bags led to an 85 per cent drop in their use by shoppers in England.[3] This suggests the tax went beyond consumers making a marginal financial decision as to whether to buy a plastic bag or not, to their appreciation that the use of plastic bags is something that should be avoided for sustainability reasons. Indeed, in England a majority (52 per cent) already supported the tax before it was introduced, and this level of support actually increased (to 60 per cent) after it was introduced (Poortinga et al., 2016).

Similarly, attempts at altering corporate behaviour have been hampered by the assumption that they are profit maximising entities that respond only to orders (through the law or regulation) or price signals. Managerial decision-making and corporate behaviour is in reality more complex, being influenced by corporate culture, social norms, peer pressure, and the behaviour of other managers and

---

3   *The Guardian*, 30 July 2016.

firms. Thus, government policy should aim to change management decision-making and corporate behaviour. This needs to be based on an appreciation of the range of drivers behind such decision-making and behaviour. Different corporate ownership structures involve different governance measures, corporate policies and practices, and decision-making and behaviours. So corporate diversity can help. Public ownership can likewise be used to create firms that will act appropriately, and it has been shown that this can have a positive knock-on effect on other firms in the sector. A wide range of policy measures can thus prove effective – and by utilising the full range, these can become self-reinforcing and synergistic (on which, see Michie and Oughton, 2011). The aim should therefore be to *alter corporate behaviour and management decision-making through a combination of legislation, regulation, taxation, and corporate diversity.*

Regarding both the above policy areas, of altering consumer and producer behaviour, Dawnay and Shah (2011) stress seven principles: other people's behaviour matters – people do many things by observing others and copying; habits are important – people do many things without consciously thinking about them; people are motivated to 'do the right thing', and there are cases when money is demotivating as it undermines people's intrinsic motivation; people's self-expectations influence how they behave – they want their actions to be in line with their values and their commitments; people are loss-averse and hang on to what they consider 'theirs'; people are bad at computation when making decisions, putting, for example, undue weight on recent events and too little weight on far-off ones; and people need to feel involved and effective to make a change – just giving people incentives and information is not necessarily enough.

10.2   Policies which are appropriate to pursue at national level

10.2.1   Industrial strategy and policy[4]

In most countries, an important component of industrial strategy has been *the use of public ownership* to provide an effective and efficient

---

4 For a discussion and advocacy of the use of industrial policy – in the context of the current state of globalisation – by the developing world in particular, following the success of such approaches by East Asian countries in the past, see Jalil (2016).

productive infrastructure, and to ensure that industries modernise and take the long view as appropriate – which often fails to happen in the private sector, which is too often focused on quarterly financial returns and short-term movements in share prices. Using public ownership for long-term investment in the productive infrastructure should be used where private ownership proves inadequate, insufficient, or uncertain. The public sector will deliver the UK's major infrastructural project referred to above, at Hinkley Point – the French and Chinese public sectors, as the UK's no longer has the capabilities. For those countries like the UK which lack a public sector with the necessary capacity and capabilities, these should be developed as part of a long-term industrial strategy.

In addition to using the public sector for major infrastructural projects, the utilities, and the productive infrastructure, public entrepreneurship can be used for high-tech innovation. When this is done, the key is to recognise that failures in such areas are an inevitable part of the innovative and entrepreneurial process, so where agreed objectives for a start-up aren't achieved, failures should be permitted, with the financial and other resources moving on to other innovative start-ups for which the only weakness is a lack of finance.

Member-owned companies – co-operatives, mutuals and employee-owned firms – should be promoted both as appropriate and useful corporate structures in their own right, and also to create a healthy degree of corporate diversity. These forms may be better suited to local and national operation than multinational, and this is to be welcomed, given the environmental benefits of localism.

10.2.2   Innovation strategy[5]

The founder of Sussex University's Science Policy Research Unit (SPRU) in the UK, the late Professor Chris Freeman documented over decades the important role of 'national systems of innovation' in those countries that enjoyed successful economic development with high rates of innovation. By this he meant a strong presence of the key factors of investment in education, skills development, research, access to long-term patient capital, industrial confidence in future demand for innovative products, and so on, along with intermediary institutions and arrangements to take full advantage of the synergies between these

---

5 For a detailed analysis of innovation policy in a global economy, see Archibugi et al. (1999a).

factors, such as for university spin-outs. It might be thought that a focus on 'national systems' is anachronistic in an era of globalisation. But actually, the greater the degree of international competition, the greater the pay-back for firms – or whole economies – that gain a competitive advantage in global markets, and being at the cutting edge of innovation is the surest way of achieving that position. Porter (1990, p. 19), for example argues that:

> Competitive advantage is created and sustained through a highly localised process. Differences in national economic structures, values, cultures, institutions and histories contribute profoundly to competitive success. The role of the home nation seems to be as strong or stronger than ever. While globalisation of competition might appear to make the nation less important, instead it seems to make it more so. With fewer impediments to trade to shelter uncompetitive domestic firms and industries, the home nation takes on growing significance because it is the source of the skills and technology that underpin competitive advantage.

That said, the key aspect of Freeman's work was the 'systems' of innovation, rather than the 'national', and while there had been countries where the above combination was deliberately promoted with good effect, such as Japan, the same point about creating and promoting these synergistic relations apply at other levels than the national, including the regional and the sectoral. Thus, a successful innovation strategy should invest in the full range of these factors that are required for the development and success of systems of innovation, nationally and at sub-national regional level, as well as within key sectors of the economy.[6]

10.2.3   Monetary and fiscal policy

'Quantitative easing' through the central bank buying bonds in the financial markets tends to inflate asset prices, to the benefit of those who own those assets (largely, the already well-off), thereby exacerbating inequality. In circumstances where such policies are required to prevent the economy slipping into recession or stagnating due to inadequate demand, such programmes should be targeted at funding renewable energy programmes and environmentally friendly infrastructure projects. This chimes with the need for fiscal and monetary policies to be used in tandem: to try to steer the economy via monetary

---

6 See for example Taylor (2016).

policy alone can be like 'pushing on a piece of string' if there is no appetite to borrow and invest.

10.3   Policies constrained by globalisation

As discussed in the previous chapter, there is scope for additional taxation of wealth and global financial speculation, and for reducing tax avoidance and evasion.

10.3.1   Wealth taxes

Piketty (2014) advocates a wealth tax to tackle the problem of inequality, along with taxes on income and inheritance. On the wealth tax, he advocates that this should be across Europe, at least. And provided it is imposed regularly – as opposed to say inheritance tax – then it can be set at a relatively low level, and yet produce significant tax revenues. An additional positive outcome is the incentive that it would create to use capital productively.

10.3.2   Taxation of global financial speculation

One of the most damaging aspects of the 'capitalism unleashed' form of globalisation created from the 1980s, as opposed to the more successful form during the 'Golden Age of Capitalism' over the previous thirty years, has been the free-for-all for global financial speculation. This should be taxed. In most cases of taxation, it is an unfortunate necessity, with the unfortunate side-effect that it may deter activities that we have no wish to deter, such as consumption (in the case of consumption taxes or VAT) or work (in the case of income taxes). But speculation damages economic activities and social outcomes. If it could be avoided, so much the better. So to the extent that such a tax reduced the activity being taxed, all well and good. And to the extent that the activity continues regardless, then at least there is some additional tax revenue.

10.3.3   Stopping tax avoidance and evasion

As discussed in the previous chapter, it is vital that tax evasion is tackled. On how to do this:

> Reining in such abuses will require many initiatives – not just measures such as automatic information exchange and beneficial ownership regis-

tration but also preventive, proactive regulation of the key players in the global haven industry; tougher penalties for tax dodgers, kleptocrats, and their enablers; mandatory offshore wealth disclosure for public officials; and stronger protection for financial whistle-blowers.

But implementing such reforms will take time. And we should not be content merely with lobbying for technical amendments to the existing hodge-podge international tax system that might succeed in reforming this system some fine day … trillions in anonymous, largely untaxed, in many cases crime-related private wealth is just sitting there, invested in relatively low-yield offshore investments. If we can figure out how to levy a modest global tax against it, or at least encourage it to return to the surface where it can be more productively invested, all this wealth might at least begin to make a contribution while we wait for the more comprehensive reform.

Our proposal involves levying a transnational Anonymous Wealth Tax (AWT) at a modest 0.5 per cent annual rate. If implemented carefully by a determined coalition of rich countries and key developing countries, even this modest rate could generate tens of billions of dollars per year – $50 billion to $60 billion, at most ten per cent of the annual income earned by these hidden offshore assets – of badly needed revenue, either directly, or by providing an incentive for anonymous wealth to come back home, where it can be invested and taxed by local authorities. (Henry, 2016a)

As discussed in the previous chapter, it should not be permitted to try to evade or avoid taxation. To do so should be treated as an attempt to subvert the law – conspiring to subvert the course of justice.

10.4   Summary of policy headings

(a)   Climate change: a Green New Deal

The overarching policy need for all countries, domestically and through international co-operation, is to pursue a Green New Deal. This needs to include investing in domestic and industrial energy efficiency to reduce the demand for energy; investing in renewables – wind, solar, hydroelectric, wave and tidal power – to meet (these reduced) energy needs; cutting transport emissions through regulation, innovation, and localisation; altering consumer behaviour through public engagement and involvement; and shifting corporate behaviour and management decision-making through the use of legislation, regulation, and taxation, and by promoting greater corporate diversity. This increased corporate diversity should include the active use of public enterprise. A small number of companies acting in environmentally friendly ways can have important knock-on effects for other companies in their networks. This is one use to which new public enterprises could be put. Increased corporate diversity should also include stronger co-operative, mutual and employee-owned sectors. Such firms may be more suited to local, regional and national operation rather than global, which is a further benefit in terms of strengthening the local in the economy – across the world.

(b) Policies which it's appropriate to pursue at national level: modernisation

There are a huge range of policy areas on which national governments can act in significant and useful ways, including for example education, health, housing, transport, and policing – in other words, almost all the areas with which electorates are most concerned. The idea of governments being constrained by globalisation has perhaps centred more on economic and particularly fiscal policy, but as argued above, the area of industrial strategy, including the use of public ownership and promoting corporate diversity, is made if anything more important in the face of increased international competition. An important element of this is to promote corporate diversity, for a dynamic and resilient economic system. That includes making active and intelligent use of public ownership, both to provide a modern and environmentally friendly productive infrastructure, and also public entrepreneurship, where a relatively small number of firms acting positively – for example in terms of sustainable development – can have a significant and positive impact on the behaviour of other firms.[7] It also includes promoting co-operatives, mutual and employee-owned businesses.[8] Similarly on the need to promote R&D and innovation, such policies are made more relevant rather than less by a more open and globalised economy. As for monetary and fiscal policies, it is precisely the global financial crisis that forced governments to pursue such policies more enthusiastically, most notably with the use of 'quantitative easing': this should in future be targeted at Green New Deal projects.

---

7 As analysed and described by Michie and Oughton (2011).

8 Zamagni and Zamagni (2010) discuss such 'member-owned' organisations in the face of globalisation. See also the global strategy of the International Co-operative Alliance.

(c) Policies constrained by globalisation: taxation

The biggest constraint might be thought to be on taxation. Ironically, leaving to one side the need for governments to raise revenues, it is argued above that to tackle three of the worst outcomes of globalisation, increased taxation would play a positive role – quite apart from the fact that this would result in increased tax revenues. First, increased inequality is corrosive for society and damaging to the economy, as a greater proportion of the wealth is likely to be hoarded when it is diverted to the already super-wealthy. Second, the diversion of economic activity away from productive activities into unproductive financial speculation. And third, the increased incidence of tax evasion and avoidance. The three main levers to tackle these problems would be the use of wealth taxes, the introduction of a transactions tax on speculative capital movement, and a crackdown on tax evasion and avoidance. Ironically, therefore, by creating these problems that call for these solutions, globalisation has created the conditions for introducing significant new tax measures that would deliver large increases in tax receipts globally.

10.5   Conclusion: yes we can

The introductory chapter referred to the detailed work done by Sutcliffe and Glyn (2011) on the actual extent of globalisation. On the basis of that analysis, they conclude that:

> . . . the exaggeration of the degree of globalisation has given rise to (or has been used to justify) a sense of impotence among many on the left. Globalisation seems to explain why national political plans always go wrong: it is because the nation state has lost independence due to globalisation. The future of left politics, therefore, seems to depend uniquely on the possibility of building an international political movement to combat globalised capital and the *de facto* international state. And since to many that prospect seems very difficult and distant, the implication is political impotence for the foreseeable future. In our opinion this fatalistic perspective would be wrong even if globalisation has advanced much further than we believe it has. It is not true that the consolidation of the national state rendered local institutions powerless and local politics redundant. No more should globalisation render redundant the politics of smaller units including the nation state. But changing global structures will tend to alter the political areas in which local or national autonomy exists. There is no reason to suppose that it will eliminate their importance.

Nevertheless, any degree of globalisation (including that which existed before it became a buzzword) does seem to us to demand greater internationalisation of political perspectives and action, whether it be international trade union action in relation to multinational corporations or international cooperation of progressives over human and civil rights, especially when these have a clear international dimension, such as questions of asylum rights, immigration rights and so on. There is a marked imbalance between the globalisation of the movement of money and things and the opposite tendency in the movement of people. It seems to demand some redress: people should be able to move more freely, and at the same time they should find it easier to acquire democratic rights when they do move. Globalisation demands now (as it always has done) that the concept of citizenship in the political process, also be globalised. The concept of international citizenship has begun to be discussed but it lags far behind the development of the ideological justification for the globalisation of money and capital markets. None of this seems to us new but globalisation at any pace makes it more urgent. It is not an alternative to national or local political action but a complement to it. (Sutcliffe and Glyn, 2011, pp. 101–102)

The sort of political action required has been illustrated above, and also by a range of authors globally, including for example the various contributors to Jacobs and Mazzucato (2016). A key focus needs to be to confront and tackle the problem of capital having become increasingly unproductive – having been diverted into financial speculation, tax avoidance and evasion, and 'rent seeking' activities which focus on changing the distribution of income in favour of the highest paid and wealthiest, rather than on creating wealth. Policy solutions need to include taxing such unproductive activities, including by restoring progressive taxation of income and wealth; introducing a tax on global financial transactions; and ending tax avoidance and evasion. Also vital is to promote corporate diversity. Such policy needs to be seen as part of and contributing to a Green New Deal, and needs to be pursued at local, regional, national and global levels.

11 Conclusion

A child of five would understand this. Send someone to fetch a child of five.

(Groucho Marx)

Even back in 1997, ten years before the 2007–2008 global financial crisis, the serious academic and commentator Dani Rodrik was asking 'Has globalisation gone too far?' – arguing that even the degree of globalisation that had occurred by that point was already triggering domestic, social and political pressure (Rodrik, 1997). But rather than pull back, at the time Rodrik was writing this, globalisation was still being cheered on by politicians, academics and practitioners alike. And then in 2007–2008 the unsustainable process proved unsustainable; the risk-sharing arrangements that were sold (quite literally) as designed to avoid a crash, crashed; and the politicians who had pronounced that government intervention was a thing of the past, that nation states could no longer act in an era of globalisation, and that nationalisation was no longer practicable and in any case the private sector was more efficient, intervened and nationalised their banks to save the private sector from itself.

There is no reason to imagine that Deutsche Bank (Germany's largest) is any better or worse than most other big global banks, but Caesar (2016) gives a nice account of how they had been reasonably low key, during the 'German miracle' of rapid growth from the 1950s to the 1970s, perhaps not wanting the limelight following their role in financing the Nazi regime, and purchasing stolen Jewish gold. Until that is the deregulation of 'capitalism unleashed', when they joined the 'greed is good' party and gorged themselves along with the rest. 'Before the housing market collapsed in the United States, in 2008, sparking a global financial crisis, Deutsche Bank created about thirty-two billion dollars' worth of collateralized debt obligations, which helped to inflate the housing bubble' (Caesar, 2016). They avoided bankruptcy during the ensuing global financial crash, although it has since been suggested that they did so only through some creative accounting.[1] They have certainly been found guilty of several disreputable practices, for which they have been fined. As reported in Chapter 9 above, this includes their role in international tax avoidance and tax evasion, which this book argues represents a major drain from productive activity, quite apart from the debilitating effect that such large scale illegal and unethical activity has on society.

> Scandals have proliferated at Deutsche Bank. Since 2008, it has paid more than nine billion dollars in fines and settlements for such improprieties as conspiring to manipulate the price of gold and silver, defrauding mortgage companies, and violating U.S. sanctions by trading in Iran, Syria, Libya, Myanmar, and Sudan. (Caesar, 2016)

Soon after that was written, Deutsche Bank was, in September 2016, fined $14 billion by the US Department of Justice for mis-selling mortgage bonds from 2005 to 2007.

11.1 The Great Recession and secular stagnation?

Almost ten years after the global financial crisis of 2007–2008, for many countries, output, employment and wage levels are barely higher than they were when the crisis struck. Even for those economies that have fared better, outcomes have been worse than in the decade prior to that global crisis. For the OECD countries, the average employment rate reached its post-crisis trough in the first quarter of 2010, with 58.6 per cent of the population (aged 15–74) employed – 2.2 percentage points lower than the employment rate had been in 2007, corresponding to 20.3 million jobs; by the end of 2015 employment was still 5.6 million lower than previously (Scarpetta, Keese and Swaim, 2016). This has led some to believe that the global economy may have entered a new era of secular stagnation – neither a return to the success in economic growth terms, at least, of the 'capitalism unleashed' era, nor the creation of a new version of the Golden Age of Capitalism arrangements which enabled a generation of relatively stable growth

---

1 'In 2010, Deutsche Bank's own staff accused it of having masked twelve billion dollars' worth of losses. Eric Ben-Artzi, a former risk analyst, was one of three whistle-blowers. He told the Securities and Exchange Commission that, had the bank's true financial health been known in 2008, it might have folded, as Lehman Brothers had. Last year, Deutsche Bank paid the S.E.C. a fifty-five-million-dollar fine but admitted no wrongdoing. Ben-Artzi told me that bank executives had incurred a tiny penalty for a huge crime. "There was cultural criminality," he said, "Deutsche Bank was structurally designed by management to allow corrupt individuals to commit fraud"' (Caesar, 2016).

and development internationally (see for example Teulings and Baldwin, 2014; and Summers, 2016 for a discussion of the implications of chronically deficient aggregate demand).

11.2   Rethinking economics

Many of the proponents of the 'capitalism unleashed' version of globalisation pursued since the 1980s – with privatisation, deregulation, demutualisation and financialisation, combined with free movement of capital across the globe – claimed the support of economic theory. In the run-up to the 2007–2008 global financial crisis, the policies and practices that were making the economic system increasingly risky, with new financial products being created for little purpose other than speculation in the pursuit of financial gain – in effect, gambling – were ironically presented as if they were spreading risks, and allowing investors to choose their own 'risk appetites' from a larger portfolio. When the inevitable occurred and the unsustainable boom came crashing down, the obvious question was why mainstream economists had not foreseen, predicted, and warned of the outcome – and, indeed, taken steps to avoid it happening. It is ironic that the person delivering this challenge – of why economists had not seen the crash coming – was the UK's Queen Elizabeth II, on a visit to the London School of Economics. (She didn't say that a five-year-old might have seen it, but she may as well have.)

Of course, there have always been critics of mainstream economics, its methods, and the resulting policy prescriptions. Since the global financial crash of 2007–2008 there has been increased disquiet at the role of mainstream economics. Manifestations of this have included the creation of the World Economics Association and the Institute for New Economic Thinking, the 'Rethinking Economics' movement and the 'Reteaching Economics' network in Britain, with similar movements and networks in other countries. My colleague Michael Kitson and I have set out in detail where we think mainstream economics goes wrong, and how economic analysis of trade, currency movements, globalisation and other such themes should be undertaken:

> There are several reasons why the economy is not amenable to simple modelling. Or rather, when it *is* subject to simple modelling – by economists – the results should be treated with a judicious degree of caution. To be specific, the results should be interpreted as applying to the particular model, not necessarily to the economy.

First, there are a huge number of economic- and non-economic factors continually interacting. Many of these interactions are two-way – where one factor will change, causing other things to change, and then these changes themselves affect the initial factor – causing a new cycle of interaction, and so on.

Second, the nature of the causal mechanisms themselves alter over time.

Third, one may sometimes find a causal mechanism from one variable to another that appears absolutely stable, so one can predict that if a certain event happens it will always be followed by the same consequence. But if something new is introduced – for example a policy intervention suggested by the economist who has discovered this stable relation – then that may well cause the previously stable correlation to break down. . . .

Fourth, many of these 'laws'. . . depend on what decisions actually come to be taken by various people in the economy (and, indeed, in other economies). . . .

And fifth, many of the things which economists are analysing . . . are simply unknowable. The answer will depend on what happens to a whole range of other factors, about which we can't be sure.

The problem, though, is not economics – it is the misuse of economics. (Kitson and Michie, 2000, pp. 3–4)

We went on to argue – in the year 2000, that:

The globalisation of the economy appears from daily news bulletins to be wreaking havoc. Yet we are told that this same globalisation precludes national governments from doing much about it. This was nicely illustrated in 1998 when the *Guardian* newspaper reported Tony Blair as arguing that globalisation had constrained the ability of any Government, such as his, from doing much about the economy, alongside a report that the arch global speculator, George Soros, was warning that global capitalism faced collapse and that Governments must intervene to stabilise and regulate the system. (Kitson and Michie, 2000, pp. 7–8)

For a discussion of the current state of economics, following the failure of mainstream economics to predict the 2007–2008 global financial crisis and subsequent recession, nor to deal adequately with the issue of globalisation, see for example Hodgson (2011), Keen (2016), and Rochon and Rossi (2016).[2]

Policy is often proposed 'to correct for market failure': the market has failed, so it is the job of government to make good. This supposes there is such a thing as 'the market'; and that it might do other than fail. Both assumptions are questionable. There is no such thing as 'the market' – markets are constructed and regulated by government and other public authorities, setting the rules and regulations. This might seem like a semantic point. But as Sawyer (1991, p. 96) has argued – in our view persuasively – the underlying assumptions of the 'market failure' idea 'is not a fruitful starting point for the analysis of a developed industrial economy':

> To argue that markets do not operate as envisaged in much of economic theory and in ways which are not socially desirable is not to argue in favour of central planning. Indeed, part of the general argument is that neither 'pure' markets nor 'pure' central planning are possible or desirable. Hodgson (1984, 1988) has postulated 'the impurity principle', which argues that 'co-existing structures are in fact necessary for the system to operate and reproduce itself through time'. Casual observation indicates that in all economies, elements of market trading and government planning co-exist, albeit in different proportions and forms. One form is generally dominant, so that we can describe an economy as being a market economy or a centrally planned one. But the counterposing of markets and planning has caused much difficulty in debates over the appropriate use of markets. Within so-called market economies, there are many non-market private arrangements which could be described as extra-market, which help to coordinate economic activity. A full appreciation of these extra-market arrangements and of the limits of the use of the market mechanism are required so that a helpful analysis of economic coordination can be developed, and for economic policies towards markets and planning to have stronger foundations than hitherto. (Sawyer, 1991, pp. 112–113)

---

2 See also the academic journals that aren't restricted to mainstream articles, such as the *Cambridge Journal of Economics*, the *Cambridge Journal of Regions, Economy & Society*, the *International Review of Applied Economics*, and the *Review of International Political Economy*.

11.3 Globalisation

A 2012 survey found that only 22 per cent of French people thought globalisation a 'good thing' for their country (*The Economist*, 23 September 2013). As the hotel worker asked George Best, 'Where did it all go wrong?'[3] In terms of globalisation:

> The enthroning of free capital mobility – especially of the short-term kind – as a policy norm by the European Union, the Organization for Economic Cooperation and Development, and the IMF was arguably the most fateful decision for the global economy in recent decades. As Harvard Business School professor Rawi Abdelal has shown, this effort was spearheaded in the late 1980s and early 1990s not by free-market ideologues, but by French technocrats such as Jacques Delors (at the European Commission) and Henri Chavranski (at the OECD), who were closely associated with the Socialist Party in France. Similarly, in the US, it was technocrats associated with the more Keynesian Democratic Party, such as Lawrence Summers, who led the charge for financial deregulation.
>
> France's Socialist technocrats appear to have concluded from the failed Mitterrand experiment with Keynesianism in the early 1980s that domestic economic management was no longer possible, and that there was no real alternative to financial globalisation. (Rodrik, 2016a)

The global economic advisor to Pimco, a global investment house with $1.5 trillion under management wrote in a research note, 'The vote in the UK is part of a wider, more global, backlash against the establishment, rising inequality and globalisation'. As Lysandrou (2011) has argued, it was that rising inequality with the exacerbation of a 'super rich elite' (the 1 per cent, or even worse the 0.1 per cent) that created the demand for the new financial products that wreaked such havoc during the 2007–2008 global financial crisis. The global crisis that was created by globalisation has in turn undermined that 'inevitable' process – not just politically, with the increased opposition as referred to above, but also in terms of its own 'progress'. Thus:

---

3 George Best was a Manchester United footballer in the 1960s, who died of alcoholism. The remark was made by the hotel worker delivering a bottle of champagne to George's hotel room, which he was sharing with the then 'Miss World', and with his gambling winnings from the evening strewn across the bed. Sadly, George used to recount the story as if nothing had gone wrong at all, despite the fact that he was by then already drinking himself to an early death.

[F]ollowing the Great Recession of 2008–09, global trade and FDI perfor-mance did not resume their accustomed growth rates, unlike in the after-math of previous recessions. Four years of flat or declining world trade to GDP ratios were experienced between 1974 and 1978, six years between 1980 and 1986 . . . and now seven years and counting since 2008. This is the longest postwar period of relative stagnation.' And 'FDI flows fell from a peak of $1.9 trillion in 2007 to $1.2 trillion in 2014.' (Hufbauer and Jung, 2016)

11.4 Public policy

It is important to have active and intelligent public policy in the areas of globalisation and innovation, for two categories of reasons. First, whether these processes will be on balance beneficial or harm-ful to regions, industrial sectors, and whole economies is not a pre-determined 'given' – it will depend in large part on the policies that governments and other public authorities pursue, and with what effectiveness. Second, to have the maximal beneficial effect, such poli-cies invariably need to be supported by and work with other syner-gistic policies, so that it will be *packages* of policies that help craft well-functioning networks of economic actors, making up productive systems that are both dynamic and resilient.[4]

Evans (1997) argues that globalisation restricts state power, but also that this is unlikely to be to a significant degree, given that national success still depends upon the capabilities of states.[5] National govern-ments do indeed have such capabilities. While to some extent, as part of the 'capitalism unleashed' process, governments have transferred power to multinational corporations, that process can and should be reversed. To the extent that sovereignty has been pooled with other nation states in order to promote co-operative action globally and regionally, this is useful and important in its own right, and should not

---

4 On the sort of policy agenda that needs to be developed to deal with the problems that capitalism unleashed has caused, and in the context of the constraints that this form of globalisation has cre-ated for populations globally, see for example Stiglitz (2015) which focuses on the US but which includes measures to tame globalisation.

5 Garrett (1998) argues in similar terms that globalisation can indeed constrain national policies politically. We would argue there are two meanings to the term constrain: one is whether govern-ments have the ability to implement their policies, which we have argued above that to a significant extent they do, but with the caveat that the policies which governments should be seeking to implement will themselves be different because of globalisation.

undermine the ability to pursue policies locally and nationally – quite the contrary, such global arrangements should indeed enable and support such local and national policy action.[6] The state has long been declared dead – just one example being Kindleberger's declaration that 'The state is just about over as an economic unit'; as indicated, there has been some pooling of sovereignty which is to be welcomed, and some transfer of power from governments to markets and the private sector, which could be reversed, but the interpretation of this as the state being over as an economic unit is misplaced – today as it was when Kindleberger declared it so almost fifty years ago (in 1969). Indeed, Corlett (2016, p. 9) argues that much of the detriment to living standards blamed on globalisation is due in fact to national governments, and they have the power and capability to deal with the problem:

> That task is about how the gains from trade are shared, not its existence, and about how public policy supports places and people affected by economic change from trade or elsewhere. Crucially it is also about recognising that domestic policy is central to determining working people's living standards even in a globalised world. Changes to trade policy, even where desirable, are not a substitute for progressive taxes and benefits, fair wage policies and sufficient house building.

What is needed is action at the local, regional, national and international levels, and appropriate forms of democratic government and governance arrangements are required for each of these levels. We need to 'think global and local, and act global and local'. (For an argument in favour of moving from 'globalisation' to 'localisation', not least for environmental reasons, see Hines, 2011). We need to remain cognisant of the fact that for the foreseeable future, national governments are going to be key players in these arrangements. Local activities and actions are important not only for pursuing appropriate arrangements at that level, but also for putting pressure on national governments, who will only be as effective as such pressure succeeds in making them.[7] As Franklin D. Roosevelt said to a group of activists who sought

---

6 The importance of considering urbanisation, alongside globalisation, is discussed by Brenner (1999); the key point is that 'place' matters, and indeed that the response to globalisation should be not just to pursue appropriate policies nationally, but at the same time to reform the global architecture, and to pursue sub-national policies regionally and locally. See also Kettl (2000), Tarrow (2001), Li and Reuveny (2003), Simmons and Elkins (2004), Swyngedouw (2004), Giavazzi and Tabellini (2005) and López-Córdova and Meissner (2008).

7 This argument for action at local levels, for example around credit unions, whilst keeping pressure on law makers, is advocated also by, for example, Mason (2015).

his support for legislation, after having listened to their arguments for some time: 'You've convinced me. Now go out and make me do it.'

This pressure needs to be for governments to implement domestically – and co-operate internationally – to deliver a new era of sustainable development. This needs to be based around a global Green New Deal. It needs to be underpinned by progressive income, wealth and capital-gains taxes, a tax on international speculative capital movements, and a crackdown on tax evasion and avoidance. It also requires an active promotion of corporate diversity, with the promotion of co-operative, employee-owned and mutual businesses, and an intelligent use of public ownership both for the provision of efficient and environmentally friendly productive and social infrastructures, and the use of public entrepreneurship to foster innovation and productive dynamism. Capital needs to be put back to work – locally, regionally, nationally and globally – in the interests of sustainable development.

Bibliography

Aldrick, Philip (2016), The euro is doomed... but Joseph Stiglitz's left-wing fantasy is not the solution, *The Times*, 6 August.

Allen, Frederick E. (2012), *Super Rich Hide $21 Trillion Offshore, Study Says*, forbes.com, 23 July (retrieved 3 January 2017).

Amato, Massimo and Luca Fantacci (2014), Back to which Bretton Woods? Liquidity and clearing as alternative principles for reforming international money, *Cambridge Journal of Economics*, Vol. 38, Number 6, pp. 1431–1452.

Anand, Sudhir and Paul Segal (2015), The Global Distribution of Income, in Anthony B. Atkinson and Francois Bourguignon (eds), *Handbook of Income Distribution*, Vol. 2A, Amsterdam: North-Holland, 937–979.

Anand, Sudhir and Paul Segal (2016), *Who are the Global Top 1%?*, International Development Institute Working Paper 2016-02, King's International Development Institute, King's College London.

Archibugi, Daniele and Jonathan Michie (1995), The globalization of technology: a new taxonomy, *Cambridge Journal of Economics*, Vol. 19, Number 1, pp. 121–140.

Archibugi, Daniele and Jonathan Michie (1997a), Technological globalisation or national systems of innovation?, *Futures*, Vol. 29, Number 2, pp. 121–137.

Archibugi, Daniele and Jonathan Michie (eds) (1997b), *Technology, Globalisation and Economic Performance*, Cambridge: Cambridge University Press.

Archibugi, Daniele and Jonathan Michie (eds) (1998), *Trade, Growth and Technical Change*, Cambridge: Cambridge University Press.

Archibugi, Daniele, Jeremy Howells and Jonathan Michie (eds) (1999a), *Innovation Policy in a Global Economy*, Cambridge: Cambridge University Press.

Archibugi, Daniele, Jeremy Howells and Jonathan Michie (1999b), Innovation systems in a global economy, *Technology Analysis & Strategic Management*, Vol. 11, Number 4, pp. 527–539.

Arestis, Philip and Malcolm Sawyer (1999), What Role for the Tobin Tax in World Economic Governance, in Jonathan Michie and John Grieve Smith (eds), *Global Instability: The Political Economy of World Economic Governance*, London: Routledge, Chapter 7.

Arestis, Philip and Malcolm Sawyer (2011), European Integration and the 'Euro Project', in J. Michie (ed.), *The Handbook of Globalisation*, 2nd edition, Cheltenham, UK and Northampton, MA, USA: Edward Elgar Publishing, Chapter 15.

Arestis, Philip and Malcolm Sawyer (2013), The Potential of Financial Transaction Taxes, in P. Arestis and M. Sawyer (eds), *Economic Policies, Governance and the New Economics*, Basingstoke: Palgrave Macmillan, 87–121.

Atkinson, Anthony Barnes (2015), *Inequality: What Can be Done?*, Cambridge, MA: Harvard University Press.

Atkinson, Anthony Barnes and Thomas Piketty (eds) (2007), *Top Income over the Twentieth Century: A Contrast Between European and English-speaking Countries*, Oxford: Oxford University Press.

Avi-Yonah, Reuven S. (2000), Globalization, tax competition, and the fiscal crisis of the welfare state, *Harvard Law Review*, Vol. 113, Number 7, pp. 1573-1676.

Bacevich, Andrew J. (2016), Ending endless war, *Foreign Affairs*, September/October (retrieved 3 January 2017 from www.foreignaffairs.com).

Bailey, David, Alex de Ruyter, Jonathan Michie and Paul Tyler (2010), Global restructuring and the auto industry, *Cambridge Journal of Regions, Economy and Society*, Vol. 3, Number 3, pp. 311-318.

Bakan, Joel (2015), The invisible hand of law: private regulation and the rule of law, *Cornell International Law Journal*, Vol. 48, Number 2, Spring, pp. 279-300.

Baldwin, Richard E. and Philippe Martin (1999), *Two Waves of Globalisation: Superficial Similarities, Fundamental Differences*, National Bureau of Economic Research, Working Paper w6904.

Barker, Tyson (2016), How TTIP lost steam, *Foreign Affairs*, 28 September (retrieved 3 January 2017 from www.foreignaffairs.com).

Blackford, George H. (2016), *Economics Should Stop Defending Milton Friedman's Pseudo-science*, evonomics.com, 29 August (retrieved 3 January 2017).

Bourguignon, Francois and Christian Morrisson (2002), Inequality among world citizens: 1820-1992, *American Economic Review*, September, pp. 727-744.

Brady, David, Jason Beckfield and Martin Seeleib-Kaiser (2005), Economic globalization and the welfare state in affluent democracies, 1975–2001, *American Sociological Review*, Vol. 70, Number 6, pp. 921-948.

Bramley, Glen, Donald Hirsch, Mandy Littlewood and David Watkins (2016), *Counting the Cost of UK Poverty*, London: Joseph Rowntree Foundation.

Braunstein, Elissa (2011), Foreign Direct Investment and Development from a Gender Perspective, in J. Michie (ed.), *The Handbook of Globalisation*, 2nd edition, Cheltenham, UK and Northampton, MA, USA: Edward Elgar Publishing, Chapter 10.

Braunstein, Elissa and Gerald Epstein (1999), Creating International Credit Rules and the Multilateral Agreement on Investment: What are the Alternatives?, in J. Michie and J. Grieve Smith (eds), *Global Instability: The Political Economy of World Economic Governance*, London and New York: Routledge, Part II, Chapter 5, 113-133.

Brenner, Neil (1999), Globalisation as reterritorialisation: the re-scaling of urban governance in the European Union, *Urban Studies*, Vol. 36, Number 3, pp. 431-451.

Brown, Phillip and Hugh Lauder (1996), Education, globalization and economic development, *Journal of Education Policy*, Vol. 11, Number 1, pp. 1-25.

Buckley, Peter J. and Pervez N. Ghauri (2004), Globalisation, economic geography and the strategy of multinational enterprises, *Journal of International Business Studies*, Vol. 35, Number 2, pp. 81-98.

Caesar, Ed (2016), Deutsche Bank's $10-billion scandal: how a scheme to help Russians secretly funnel money offshore unraveled, *The New Yorker*, 29 August.

Calvo, Guillermo A. and Enrique G. Mendoza (2000), Rational contagion and the globalization of securities markets, *Journal of International Economics*, Vol. 51, Number 1, pp. 79–113.

Campbell, Douglas and Lester Lusher (2016), *Drivers of Inequality: Trade Shocks Versus Top Marginal Tax Rates*, voxeu.org, 8 September (retrieved 3 January 2017).

Cantwell, John (1995), The globalisation of technology: what remains of the product cycle model?, *Cambridge Journal of Economics*, Vol. 19, Number 1, pp. 155–174.

Cantwell, John and Rajneesh Narula (2001), The eclectic paradigm in the global economy, *International Journal of the Economics of Business*, Vol. 8, Number 2, pp. 155–172.

Chang, Ha-Joon (2002), *Kicking Away the Ladder – Development Strategy in Historical Perspective*, London: Anthem Press.

Chang, Ha-Joon (2011), Kicking Away the Ladder – Globalisation and Economic Development in Historical Perspective, in J. Michie (ed.), *The Handbook of Globalisation*, 2nd edition, Cheltenham, UK and Northampton, MA, USA: Edward Elgar Publishing, Chapter 24.

Christmann, Petra and Glen Taylor (2001), Globalization and the environment: determinants of firm self-regulation in China, *Journal of International Business Studies*, Vol. 32, Number 3, pp. 439–458.

Christopherson, C., J. Michie and P. Tyler (2008), Innovation, networks and knowledge exchange, *Cambridge Journal of Regions, Economy and Society*, Vol. 1, Number 2, pp. 165–173.

Christopherson, Susan, Michael Kitson and Jonathan Michie (2010), Regional resilience: theoretical and empirical perspectives, *Cambridge Journal of Regions, Economy and Society*, Vol. 3, Number 1, pp. 3–10.

Colantone, Italo and Piero Stanig (2016), *The Real Reason the UK Voted for Brexit? Jobs Lost to Chinese Competition*, Bocconi University, washingtonpost.com (retrieved 3 January 2017).

Collier, Stephen J. and Andrew Lakoff (2008), Distributed preparedness: the spatial logic of domestic security in the United States, *Environment and Planning D: Society and Space*, Vol. 26, Number 1, pp. 7–28.

Corlett, Adam (2016), *Examining an Elephant: Globalisation and the Lower Middle Class of the Rich World*, London: Resolution Foundation.

Craypo, Charles and Frank Wilkinson (2011), The low road to competitive failure: immigrant labour and emigrant jobs in the US, in J. Michie (ed.), *The Handbook of Globalisation*, 2nd edition, Cheltenham, UK and Northampton, MA, USA: Edward Elgar Publishing, Chapter 17.

Cruz, Marcio, James Foster, Bryce Quillin and Philip Schellekens (2015), *Ending Extreme Poverty and Sharing Prosperity: Progress and Policies*, World Bank Policy Research Note PRN/15/03, Washington DC.

David, P. and D. Foray (1995), Accessing and expanding the science and technology knowledge base, *Science Technology Industry Review*, Number 16, pp. 13–68.

Dawnay, Emma and Hetan Shah (2011), Behavioural Economics: Seven Key Principles for Environmental Policy, in S. Dietz, J. Michie and C. Oughton (eds), *The Political Economy of the Environment*, London: Routledge, Part I, Chapter 4.

Deacon, Bob (2000), Eastern European welfare states: the impact of the politics of globalization, *Journal of European Social Policy*, Vol. 10, Number 2, pp. 146–161.

DeMartino, George (2000), *Global Economy, Global Justice: Theoretical Objections and Policy Alternatives to Neoliberalism*, London: Routledge.

DeMartino, George (2011), Free Trade or Social Tariffs?, in J. Michie (ed.), *The Handbook of Globalisation*, 2nd edition, Cheltenham, UK and Northampton, MA, USA: Edward Elgar Publishing, Chapter 26.

DeMartino, George and Stephen Cullenberg (1994), Beyond the competitiveness debate: an internationalist Agenda, *Social Text*, Number 41, pp. 11–40.

Derrida, Jacques (1994), *Specters of Marx: State of the Debt, the Work of Mourning and the New Internationalism*, London: Routledge.

Dietz, Simon, Jonathan Michie and Christine Oughton (eds) (2011), *The Political Economy of the Environment: An Interdisciplinary Approach*, London: Routledge.

Dollar, David and Aart Kraay (2004), Trade, growth, and poverty, *The Economic Journal*, Vol. 114, Number 493, pp. F22–F49.

Dosi, G. (1988), Source, procedures and microeconomic effects of innovation, *Journal of Economic Literature*, Number 36, pp. 1126–1171.

Dreher, Axel (2006), Does globalization affect growth? Evidence from a new index of globalization, *Applied Economics*, Vol. 38, Number 10, pp. 1091–1110.

Dunning, John H. (1973), The determinants of international production. *Oxford Economic Papers*, Vol. 25, Number 3, pp. 289–336.

Eatwell, J. and L. Taylor (2000), *Global Finance at Risk: The Case for International Regulation*, Cambridge: Polity Press.

Eichengreen, Barry (2015), *The Great Depression, The Great Recession, and the Uses – and Misuses of History*, Oxford: Oxford University Press.

Eichengreen, Barry (2016), *Airing the IMF's Dirty Laundry*, project-syndicate.org, 12 August (retrieved 3 January 2017).

Elliott, Larry (2016), Banking crisis blamed for pay freeze decade, *The Guardian*, 14 July.

Epstein, Gerald (2011), The Role and Control of Multinational Corporations in the World Economy, in J. Michie (ed.), *The Handbook of Globalisation*, 2nd edition, Cheltenham, UK and Northampton, MA, USA: Edward Elgar Publishing, Chapter 9.

Evans, Peter (1997), The eclipse of the state? Reflections on stateness in an era of globalization, *World Politics*, Vol. 50, Number 1, pp. 62–87.

Farlow, Andrew (2013), *Crash and Beyond: Causes and Consequences of the Global Financial Crisis*, Oxford: Oxford University Press.

Fleming, Sam and Barney Jopson (2016), US companies braced for tax shake-up as Apple feud escalates, *Financial Times*, 25 August.

Florida, Richard (1997), The globalization of R&D: results of a survey of foreign-affiliated R&D laboratories in the USA, *Research Policy*, Vol. 26, Number 1, pp. 85–103.

Forbes, Peter (2016), A guide to the latest developments as the transition to renewable energy gains speed up (review of *The Switch: How Solar, Storage and New Tech Means Cheap Power for All*, by Chris Goodall), *The Guardian*, 30 July.

Foxon, Timothy J., Jonathan Michie, Jonathan Köhler and Christine Oughton (2013), Towards a new complexity economics for sustainability, *Cambridge Journal of Economics*, Vol. 37, Number 1, pp. 187–208.

Frankel, Jeffrey A. and David Romer (1999), Does trade cause growth?, *American Economic Review*, Vol. 89, Number 3, pp. 379-399.

Freeman, Christopher (1994), The economics of technical change, *Cambridge Journal of Economics*, Vol. 18, Number 5, pp. 463-514.

Freeman, Christopher (1997), The 'National System of Innovation' in Historical Perspective, in Daniele Archibugi and Jonathan Michie (eds), *Technology, Globalization and Economic Performance*, Cambridge: Cambridge University Press, Chapter 2.

Friedman, T.L. (2005), *The World is Flat: A Brief History of the Twenty-First Century*, New York: Farrar, Straus and Giroux.

Fukuyama, Francis (1989), The end of history, *The National Interest*, Summer.

Fukuyama, Francis (1992), *The End of History and the Last Man*, New York: Free Press.

Galbraith, James (2016), *Welcome to the Poisoned Chalice*, New Haven, CT: Yale University Press.

Garrett, Geoffrey (1998), Global markets and national politics: collision course or virtuous circle?, *International Organization*, Vol. 52, Number 4, pp. 787-824.

Giavazzi, Francesco and Guido Tabellini (2005), Economic and political liberalizations, *Journal of Monetary Economics*, Vol. 52, Number 7, pp. 1297-1330.

Godley, Wynne (1993), Foreword, to Michael Kitson and Jonathan Michie, *Coordinated Deflation: The Tale of Two Recessions*, London: Full Employment Forum.

Goldberg, Pinelopi Koujianou and Nina Pavcnik (2007), Distributional effects of globalization in developing countries. *Journal of Economic Literature*, Vol. 45, Number 1, pp. 39-82.

Goldin, Ian and Chris Kutarna (2016a), *Age of Discovery: Navigating the Risks and Rewards of Our New Renaissance*, London: St Martin's Press and Bloomsbury.

Goldin, Ian and Chris Kutarna (2016b), *Pessimism is Rife, Optimism Naïve. Activism is the Best Tool for Now*, theconversation.com, 3 August (retrieved 3 January 2017).

Goodall, Chris (2016), *The Switch: How Solar, Storage and New Tech Means Cheap Power for All*, London: Profile Books.

Goodwin, Matthew and Robert Ford (2013), *Revolt on the Right: Explaining Support for the Radical Right in Britain*, London: Routledge.

Goyal, S. (2007), *Connections: An Introduction to the Economics of Networks*, Princeton, NJ: Princeton University Press.

Grossman, Gene M. and Alan B. Krueger (1991), *Environmental Impacts of a North American Free Trade Agreement*, National Bureau of Economic Research, Working Paper w3914.

Haldane, Andrew (2016), I sympathise with savers but jobs must come first, *Sunday Times*, 14 August.

Harcourt, Wendy (2014), The future of capitalism: a consideration of alternatives, *Cambridge Journal of Economics*, Vol. 38, Number 6, pp. 1307-1328.

Harris, Laurence and Jonathan Michie (1998), The effects of globalization on policy formation in South Africa, Paper presented to Economic Policy Institute conference, Washington DC and published in D. Baker, G. Epstein and R. Pollin (eds), *Globalization and Progressive Economic Policy*, Cambridge: Cambridge University Press, 1998.

Harvey, David (2009), The art of rent: globalisation, monopoly and the commodification of culture, *Socialist Register*, Vol. 38, pp. 93–110.

Heintz, James (2011), Global Labor Standards: Their Impact and Implementation, in J. Michie (ed.), *The Handbook of Globalisation*, 2nd edition, Cheltenham, UK and Northampton, MA, USA: Edward Elgar Publishing, Chapter 13.

Henderson, Jeffrey, Peter Dicken, Martin Hess, Neil Coe and Henry Wai-Chung Yeung (1992), Global production networks and the analysis of economic development, *Review of International Political Economy*, Vol. 9, Number 3, pp. 436–464.

Henry, James S. (2016a), Taxing tax havens: how to respond to the Panama Papers, *Foreign Affairs*, 12 April (retrieved 3 January 2017 from www.foreignaffairs. com).

Henry, James S. (2016b), *More Than $12 Trillion Stuffed Offshore, From Developing Countries Alone*, Tax Justice Network (retrieved 3 January 2017 from www.taxjustice. net).

Hines, Colin (2011), Time to Replace Globalisation with Localisation, in J. Michie (ed.), *The Handbook of Globalisation*, 2nd edition, Cheltenham, UK and Northampton, MA, USA: Edward Elgar Publishing, Chapter 25.

Hirst, Paul and Grahame Thompson (1992), The problem of globalization: international economic relations, national economic management, and the formation of trading blocs, *Economy and Society*, Vol. 21, Number 4, pp. 357–396.

Hirst, Paul and Grahame Thompson (1994), Globalization, foreign direct investment and international economic governance, *Organization*, Vol. 1, Number 2, pp. 277–303.

Hirst, Paul and Grahame Thompson (2011), The Future of Globalisation, in J. Michie (ed.), *The Handbook of Globalisation*, 2nd edition, Cheltenham, UK and Northampton, MA, USA: Edward Elgar Publishing, Chapter 1.

Hodgson, Geoffrey M. (1984), *The Democratic Economy*, London: Penguin.

Hodgson, Geoffrey M. (1988), *Economics and Institutions*, Oxford: Polity Press.

Hodgson, Geoffrey M. (2011), The Great Crash of 2008 and the Reform of Economics, in J. Michie (ed.), *The Handbook of Globalisation*, 2nd edition, Cheltenham, UK and Northampton, MA, USA: Edward Elgar Publishing, Chapter 28.

Hodgson, Geoffrey M. (2015), *Conceptualizing Capitalism: Institutions, Evolution, Future*, Chicago, IL: University of Chicago Press.

Hodgson, Geoffrey M. (2016), *How Capitalism Actually Generates More Inequality: Why Extending Markets or Increasing Competition won't Reduce Inequality*, evonomics. com, 11 August (retrieved 3 January 2017).

Howells, Jeremy (2011), Innovation and Globalisation: A Systems of Innovation Perspective, in J. Michie (ed.), *The Handbook of Globalisation*, 2nd edition, Cheltenham, UK and Northampton, MA, USA: Edward Elgar Publishing, Chapter 5.

Howells, Jeremy and Jonathan Michie (1998), Technological competitiveness in an international arena, *The International Journal of the Economics of Business*, Vol. 5, Number 3, pp. 279–293.

Hufbauer, Gary Clyde and Euijin Jung (2016), *Why Has Trade Stopped Growing? Not Much Liberalization and Lots of Micro-Protection*, Peterson Institute for International Economics, 23 March (retrieved 3 January 2017 from www.piie.com).

Iammarino, Simona and Jonathan Michie (1998), The scope of technological globalisation, *The International Journal of the Economics of Business*, Vol. 5, Number 3, pp. 335–353.

Ietto-Gillies, Grazia (2011), The Role of Transnational Corporations in the Globalisation Process, in J. Michie (ed.), *The Handbook of Globalisation*, 2nd edition, Cheltenham, UK and Northampton, MA, USA: Edward Elgar Publishing, Chapter 8.

Independent Evaluation Office (IEO) of the IMF (2016), *The IMF and the Crisis in Greece, Ireland, and Portugal: An Evaluation by the Independent Evaluation Office*, Washington, DC: IMF Publication Services.

Inglehart, Ronald (2000), Globalization and postmodern values, *Washington Quarterly*, Vol. 23, Number 1, pp. 215–228.

International Monetary Fund (IMF) (1999), *World Economic Outlook. International Financial Contagion: May*, Washington, DC: IMF.

International Monetary Fund (IMF) (2016), *World Economic Outlook. Too Slow for Too Long: April*, Washington, DC: IMF.

Iversen, Torben and Thomas R. Cusack (2000), The causes of welfare state expansion: deindustrialization or globalization?, *World Politics*, Vol. 52, Number 3, pp. 313–349.

Izurieta, A. and A. Singh (2010), Does fast growth in India and China help or harm US workers?, *Journal of Human Development and Capabilities*, Vol. 11, Number 1, pp. 115–141.

Jackson, M.O. (2008), *Social and Economic Networks*, Princeton, NJ: Princeton University Press.

Jackson, Tim (2011), Confronting Consumption: Challenges for Economics and for Policy, in S. Dietz, J. Michie and C. Oughton (eds), *The Political Economy of the Environment*, London: Routledge, Part III, Chapter 10.

Jacobs, Michael and Mariana Mazzucato (eds) (2016), *Rethinking Capitalism: Economics and Policy for Sustainable and Inclusive Growth*, London: Wiley-Blackwell, in association with *The Political Quarterly*.

Jalil, Mohammad Muaz (2016), Industrial policy in the 21st century: merits, demerits, and how can we make it work, *Real World Economics Review*, Number 76, September, pp. 109–123.

Jenkins, Rhys (2005), Globalization, corporate social responsibility and poverty, *International Affairs (Royal Institute of International Affairs 1944–)*, Vol. 81, Number 3, pp. 525–540.

Kahn, Yasmin (2015), *The Raj at War: A People's History of India's Second World War*, London: Bodley Head.

Kalecki, Michal (1943), Political Aspects of Full Employment, in *Selected Essays on the Dynamics of the Capitalist Economy*, Cambridge: Cambridge University Press, 1971, Part III, Chapter 12.

Kaplinsky, Raphael (2000), Globalisation and unequalisation: what can be learned from value chain analysis?, *Journal of Development Studies*, Vol. 37, Number 2, pp. 117–146.

Kaufman, Robert R. and Alex Segura-Ubiergo (2001), Globalization, domestic politics, and social spending in Latin America: a time-series cross-section analysis, 1973–97, *World Politics*, Vol. 53, Number 4, pp. 553–587.

Kay, John (2009), *The Long and Short of It*, London: The Erasmus Press.

Keen, Steve (2016), *The Slowly Changing Resistance of Economists to Change*, forbes.com, 13 August (retrieved 3 January 2017).

Kettl, Donald F. (2000), The transformation of governance: globalization, devolution, and the role of government, *Public Administration Review*, Vol. 60, Number 6, pp. 488-497.

Keynes, John Maynard (1919), *The Economic Consequences of the Peace*, New York: Harcourt, Brace and Howe.

Keynes, John Maynard (1925), *The Economic Consequences of Mr. Churchill*, London: L&V Woolf at the Hogarth Press.

Keynes, John Maynard (1933), National self-sufficiency, 1933, *The New Statesman* (UK) and *The Yale Review* (US).

Keynes, John Maynard (1936), *The General Theory of Employment, Interest and Money*, London: Palgrave Macmillan (2007 edition).

Keynes, John Maynard (1940), *How to Pay for the War*, London: Macmillan.

Khan, Yasmin (2015), *The Raj at War: A People's History of India's Second World War*, London: Bodley Head.

Kindleberger, Charles (1969), *American Business Abroad: Six Lectures on Direct Investment*, Cambridge, MA: MIT Press.

Kitson, Michael and Jonathan Michie (1995), Conflict, cooperation and change: the political economy of trade and trade policy, *Review of International Political Economy*, Vol. 2, Number 4, pp. 632-657.

Kitson, Michael and Jonathan Michie (2000), *The Political Economy of Competitiveness: Essays on Employment, Public Policy and Corporate Performance*, London: Routledge.

Kleinknecht, Alfred and Jan ter Wengel (1998), The myth of economic globalization, *Cambridge Journal of Economics*, Vol. 22, Number 5, September, pp. 637-647.

Koenig-Archibugi, Mathias (2011), Global Governance, in J. Michie (ed.), *The Handbook of Globalisation*, 2nd edition, Cheltenham, UK and Northampton, MA, USA: Edward Elgar Publishing, Chapter 19.

Komlos, John (2016), *How Bailouts, Deregulation, and Reaganomics Led to the Rise of Donald Trump*, evonomics.com, 14 August (retrieved 3 January 2017).

Korpi, Walter and Joakim Palme (2003), New politics and class politics in the context of austerity and globalization: welfare state regress in 18 countries, 1975-95, *The American Political Science Review*, Vol. 97, Number 3, pp. 425-446.

Kose, M. Ayhan, Eswar Prasad, Kenneth Rogoff and Shang-Jin Wei (2009), Financial globalization: a reappraisal, *IMF Staff Papers*, Vol. 56, Number 1, pp. 8-62.

Krugman, Paul (1979), Increasing returns, monopolistic competition, and international trade, *Journal of International Economics*, Vol. 9, Number 4, pp. 469-479.

Krugman, Paul and Anthony J. Venables (1995), *Globalization and the Inequality of Nations*, National Bureau of Economic Research, Working Paper w5098, pp. 857-880.

Kuemmerle, Walter (1999), Foreign direct investment in industrial research in the pharmaceutical and electronics industries – results from a survey of multinational firms, *Research Policy*, Vol. 28, Number 2, pp. 179-193.

Laeven, L. and F. Valencia (2008), *Systemic Banking Crises: A New Database*, IMF Working Paper No. 224, November.

Lanchester, John (2016), Brexit blues, *London Review of Books*, Vol. 38, Number 15, 28 July, pp. 3–6.

Lankester, T. (2009), Commentary. The banking crisis and inequality, *World Economics*, Vol. 10, Number 1, January–March.

Lee, Eddy (1997), Globalization and labour standards: a review of issues, *International Labour Review*, Vol. 136, Number 2, pp. 173–189.

Lee, Eddy and Marco Vivarelli (2006), The social impact of globalization in the developing countries, *International Labour Review*, Vol. 145, Number 3, pp. 167–184.

Lee, Simon (2009), *Boom to Bust: The Politics and Legacy of Gordon Brown*, Oxford: OneWorld.

Lee, Simon (2011), The Political Economy of the Third Way: The Relationship Between Globalisation and National Economic Policy, in J. Michie (ed.), *The Handbook of Globalisation*, 2nd edition, Cheltenham, UK and Northampton, MA, USA: Edward Elgar Publishing, Chapter 20.

Leijonhufvud, Axel (2009), Out of the corridor: Keynes and the crisis, *Cambridge Journal of Economics*, Vol. 33, Number 4, July, pp. 741–757.

Li, Quan and Rafael Reuveny (2003), Economic globalization and democracy: an empirical analysis, *British Journal of Political Science*, Vol. 33, Number 1, pp. 29–54.

López-Córdova, J. Ernesto and Christopher M Meissner (2008), The impact of international trade on democracy: a long-run perspective, *World Politics*, Vol. 60, Number 4, pp. 539–575.

Lundvall, B-A (ed.) (1992), *National Systems of Innovation*, London: Pinter.

Lysandrou, Photis (2011), Global Inequality and the Global Financial Crisis: The New Transmission Mechanism, in J. Michie (ed.), *The Handbook of Globalisation*, 2nd edition, Cheltenham, UK and Northampton, MA, USA: Edward Elgar Publishing, Chapter 27.

Marcuzzo, M.D. and A. Rosselli (2011), Sraffa and his arguments against 'marginalism', *Cambridge Journal of Economics*, Vol. 35, pp. 219–231.

Marglin, Stephen A. and Juliet B. Schor (eds) (1992), *The Golden Age of Capitalism: Reinterpreting the Postwar Experience*, Oxford: Oxford University Press.

Marshall, Alfred (1920), *Principles of Economics*, 8th edition, London: Macmillan.

Martin, Ron (2016), Divergent urban economic development: reflections on a tale of two cities, *Regional Policy*, Vol. 50, Number 9, pp. 1623–1627.

Marx, Karl (1867), *Capital: A Critique of Political Economy*, Moscow: Progress Publisher, www.marxists.org/archive/marx/works/download/pdf/Capital-Volume-I. pdf (retrieved 13 January 2017).

Mason, Paul (2015), *PostCapitalism: A Guide to our Future*, London: Penguin.

Mayer, Colin (2013), *Firm Commitment: Why the Corporation is Failing Us and How to Restore Trust in it*, Oxford: Oxford University Press.

Mazzucato, Mariana (2013), *The Entrepreneurial State: Debunking Public vs. Private Sector Myths*, London: Anthem Press.

McMillan, Margaret S. and Dani Rodrik (2014), Globalization, structural change and productivity growth – with an update on Africa, *World Development*, Vol. 63, pp. 11–32.

Melitz, Marc J. (2003), The impact of trade on intra-industry reallocations and aggregate industry productivity, *Econometrica*, Vol. 71, Number 6, pp. 1695–1725.

Michie, Jonathan (1997), Economic Policy in the Post-Apartheid South Africa, in P. Arestis, G. Palma and M. Sawyer (eds), *Markets, Unemployment and Economic Policy*, Routledge, Chapter 39.

Michie, Jonathan (1998), Economic Consequences of EMU for Britain, in B. Moss and J. Michie (eds), *The Single European Currency in National Perspective: A Community in Crisis?*, London: Macmillan (paperback edition, 1999), Chapter 2.

Michie, Jonathan (1999), *Currency Speculation: The Case for Reform, and the Need for a Global Response*, The 1999 Syarahan Perdana Lecture, The Prime Minister of Malaysia Fellowship Exchange Program, Kuala Lumpar.

Michie, Jonathan (2002), Foreign direct investment and human capital enhancement in developing countries, *Competition & Change*, Vol. 6, Number 4, pp. 363-372.

Michie, Jonathan (2015), The Economy, Financial Stability and Sustainable Growth, in Jonathan Michie and Cary L. Cooper (eds), *Why the Social Sciences Matter*, London: Palgrave Macmillan, Chapter 6, 92-110.

Michie, Jonathan and John Grieve Smith (eds) (1999), *Global Instability: The Political Economy of World Economic Governance*, London: Routledge.

Michie, Jonathan and Christine Oughton (2011), Managerial, Institutional and Evolutionary Approaches to Environmental Economics: Theoretical and Policy Implications, in Simon Dietz, Jonathan Michie and Christine Oughton (eds), *The Political Economy of the Environment: An Interdisciplinary Approach*, London: Routledge, Chapter 3, 44-73.

Michie, Jonathan and Christine Oughton (2013), *Measuring Diversity in Financial Services Markets: A Diversity Index*, Working Paper 097_DP113. The Centre for Financial and Management Studies, SOAS, University of London.

Michie, Jonathan and Christine Oughton (2014), *Corporate diversity in financial services – an updated diversity index*, Building Societies Association, November (retrieved 3 January 2017 from www.bsa.org.uk).

Michie, Jonathan, Christine Oughton and Antonello Zanfei (2002), Globalisation, Growth and Employment, *Journal of Interdisciplinary Economics*, Vol. 13, Numbers 1-3, pp. 1-11.

Michie, Jonathan and Vishnu Padayachee (eds) (1997), *The Political Economy of South Africa's Transition – Policy Perspectives in the late 1990s*, London: Dryden Press.

Michie, Jonathan and Vishnu Padayachee (1998), Three years after apartheid: growth, employment and redistribution? *Cambridge Journal of Economics*, Vol. 22, Number 5, pp. 623-635.

Michie, Jonathan and Chris Rowley (2014), Mutuality in the Asia Pacific region, *Asia Pacific Business Review*, Vol. 20, Number 3, pp. 506-511.

Michie, Jonathan and Frank Wilkinson (1995), Wages, government policy and unemployment, *Review of Political Economy*, Vol. 7, Number 2, April, pp. 133-149.

Michie, Jonathan, Joseph Blasi and Carlo Borzaga (eds) (2017), *Handbook of Co-operative and Mutual Business*, Oxford: Oxford University Press.

Michie, Jonathan, Christine Oughton and Matias Ramirez (2002), Globalisation and economic performance, *Journal of Interdisciplinary Economics*, Vol. 13, Numbers 1-3, pp. 165-183.

Milanovic, Branko (2016), *Global Inequality: A New Approach for the Age of Globalization*, Cambridge, MA: Harvard University Press.

Milne, Seumas (2013), *The Revenge of History: The Battle for the Twenty-first Century*, London: Verso Books.

Milner, Helen V. and Keiko Kubota (2005), Why the move to free trade? Democracy and trade policy in the developing countries, *International Organization*, Vol. 59, Number 1, pp. 107–143.

Mirowski, Philip (2014), *The Political Movement that Dared not Speak its own Name: The Neoliberal Thought Collective Under Erasure*, Institute for New Economic Thinking, Working Paper No. 23, ineteconomics.org/workingpapers.

Mockel, Peter (2016), *Energy Storage: A Critical Piece of the Power Puzzle*, blogs.worldbank.org, 28 July (retrieved 3 January 2017).

Monbiot, George (2016), *Was the Rise of Neoliberalism the Root Cause of Extreme Inequality?*, evonomics.com (retrieved 3 January 2017).

Mundell, Robert A. (1961), A theory of optimum currency areas, *The American Economic Review*, Vol. 51, Number 4, pp. 657–665.

Narula, Rajneesh and John H. Dunning (2000), Industrial development, globalization and multinational enterprises: new realities for developing countries, *Oxford Development Studies*, Vol. 28, Number 2, pp. 141–167.

Nelson, R.R. (ed.) (1993), *National Innovation Systems*, Oxford: Oxford University Press.

New Economics Foundation (2008), *A Green New Deal: Joined-Up Policies to Tackle the Triple Crunch of the Credit Crisis, Climate Change and High Oil Prices*, London: NEF.

Nicholls, Alex and Benjamin Huybrechts (2017), Fair Trade and Co-operatives, in J. Michie et al. (eds), *A Handbook of Co-operative and Mutual Business*, Oxford: Oxford University Press, Chapter 32.

Nolan, Brian, Max Roser and Stefan Thewissen (2016), *Stagnating Median Incomes Despite Economic Growth: Explaining the Divergence in 27 OECD Countries*, voxeu.org (retrieved 3 January 2017).

O'Brien, Karen L. and Robin M. Leichenko (2000), Double exposure: assessing the impacts of climate change within the context of economic globalization, *Global Environmental Change*, Vol. 10, Number 3, pp. 221–232.

Ormerod, Paul (2016), *The Future of Economics Uses the Science of Real-Life Social Networks*, evonomics.com (retrieved 3 January 2017).

Ostry, Jonathan D., Prakash Loungani and Davide Furceri (2016), Neoliberalism: Oversold?, IMF, *Finance and Development*, Vol. 53, Number 2, June.

Ownership Commission (2012), *Plurality, Stewardship and Engagement: The Report from the Commission on Ownership*, London: Mutuo.

Padayachee, Vishnu (1997), The Evolution of South Africa's International Financial Relations and Policy, 1985–1995, in Jonathan Michie and Vishnu Padayachee (eds), *The Political Economy of South Africa's Transition – Policy Perspectives in the late 1990s*, London: Dryden Press, Part I, Chapter 2.

Panic, Mica (2011), A New 'Bretton Woods' System, in J. Michie (ed.), *The Handbook of Globalisation*, 2nd edition, Cheltenham, UK and Northampton, MA, USA: Edward Elgar Publishing, Chapter 23.

Patel, Pari (1995), Localised production of technology for global markets. *Cambridge Journal of Economics*, Vol. 19, Number 1, pp. 141–153.

Patel, Pari and Modesto Vega (1999), Patterns of internationalisation of corporate technology: location vs. home country advantages, *Research Policy*, Vol. 28, Number 2, pp. 145–155.

Patel, Parimal and Keith Pavitt (1991), Large firms in the production of the world's technology: an important case of 'non-globalisation', *Journal of International Business Studies*, Vol. 22, Number 1, pp. 1–21.

Perraton, Jonathan (2011), The Scope and Implications of Globalisation, in J. Michie (ed.), *The Handbook of Globalisation*, 2nd edition, Cheltenham, UK and Northampton, MA, USA: Edward Elgar Publishing, Chapter 3.

Pieterse, Jan Nederveen (1994), Globalisation as hybridization, *International Sociology*, Vol. 9, Number 2, pp. 161–184.

Piketty, Thomas (2014), *Capital in the Twenty-First Century*, Cambridge, MA: Harvard University Press.

Poortinga, Wouter, Elena Sautkina and Gregory Thomas (2016), The 5p carrier bag charge has paved the way for other waste reduction policies, theconversation.com, 1 October (retrieved 3 January 2016).

Porter, Michael (1990), *The Competitive Advantage of Nations*, New York, Free Press/ Macmillan.

Raworth, Kate (2017), *Doughnut Economics: seven ways to think like a 21st century economist*, Random House (UK) and Chelsea Green (US).

Read, Carveth (1898), *Logic, deductive and inductive*, London: Grant Richards.

Redding, Gordon and Antony Drew (2016), Dealing with the complexity of causes of societal innovativeness: social enabling and disabling mechanisms and the case of China, *Journal of Interdisciplinary Economics*, Vol. 28, Number 2, pp. 107–136.

Richardson, Louise (2006), *What Terrorists Want: Understanding the Enemy, Containing the Threat*, London: Random House.

Richter, Felix (2015), *US Tech Companies Hoard Billions in Offshore Tax Havens*, statista.com, 14 October (retrieved 3 January 2017).

Rieger, Elmar and Stephan Leibfried (1998), Welfare state limits to globalization. *Politics & Society*, Vol. 26. Number 3, pp. 363–391.

Rivera-Batiz, Luis A. and Paul M. Romer (1991), Economic integration and endogenous growth, *The Quarterly Journal of Economics*, Vol. 106, Number 2, pp. 531–555.

Roach, Stephen S. (2016), The Globalization Disconnect, project-syndicate.org, 25 July (retrieved 3 January 2017).

Robinson, Guy M. and Doris A. Carson (eds) (2015), *Handbook on the Globalisation of Agriculture*, Cheltenham, UK and Northampton, MA, USA: Edward Elgar Publishing.

Rodrik, Dani (1996), *Why Do More Open Economies Have Bigger Governments?*, National Bureau of Economic Research, Working Paper 5537.

Rodrik, Dani (1997), Has globalization gone too far?, *California Management Review*, Vol. 39, Number 3, pp. 29–53.

Rodrik, Dani (2016a), *The Abdication of the Left*, project-syndicate, 11 July (retrieved 3 January 2017).

Rodrik, Dani (2016b), *The False Promise of Global Governance*, project-syndicate, 11 August (retrieved 3 January 2017).

Rochon, Louis-Philippe and Sergio Rossi (2016), *An Introduction to Macroeconomics: A Heterodox Approach to Economic Analysis*, Cheltenham, UK and Northampton, MA, USA: Edward Elgar Publishing.

Rosenberg, N. (1982), *Inside the Black Box: Technology and Economics*, Cambridge: Cambridge University Press.

Rosenberg, N. (1994), *Exploring the Black Box*, Cambridge: Cambridge University Press.

Rowley, Chris and Jonathan Michie (2014), Differing forms of capital: setting the scene for mutuality and co-operation in the Asia Pacific Region, *Asia Pacific Business Review*, Vol. 20, Number 3, pp. 322–329.

Rudra, Nita (2002), Globalization and the decline of the welfare state in less-developed countries, *International Organization*, Vol. 56, Number 2, pp. 411–445.

Rudra, Nita (2005), Globalization and the strengthening of democracy in the developing world, *American Journal of Political Science*, Vol. 49, Number 4, pp. 704–730.

Ruggie, John Gerard (1982), International regimes, transactions, and change: embedded liberalism in the postwar economic order, *International Organization*, Vol. 36, Number 2, pp. 379–415.

Ruhs, Martin (2013), *The Price of Rights: Regulating International Labor Migration*, Princeton, NJ: Princeton University Press.

Ruhs, Martin (2016a), The rights of migrant workers: economics, politics and ethics, *International Labour Review*, Vol. 155, Number 2, pp. 283–296.

Ruhs, Martin (2016b), Protecting the Rights of Temporary Migrant Workers: Ideals versus Reality, in Joanna Howe and Rosemary Owens (eds), *Temporary Labour Migration in the Global Era: The Regulatory Challenges*, London: Bloomsbury, Chapter 14, 299–325.

Sawyer, Malcolm (1991), Analysing the Operation of Market Economies in the Spirit of Kaldor and Kalecki, in Jonathan Michie (ed.), *The Economics of Restructuring and Intervention*, Aldershot, UK and Brookfield, VT, MA, USA: Edward Elgar Publishing, Chapter 6, 96–115.

Scarpetta, Stefano, Mark Keese and Paul Swaim (2016) *Back in Work, Still Out of Pocket: Labour Market Recovery Since the Great Recession*, voxeu.org, July 25 (retrieved 1 August 2016).

Scott, Allen J. and Michael Storper (2003), Regions, globalization, development, *Regional Studies*, Vol. 37, Numbers 6 and 7, pp. 579–593.

Sensier, Marianne, Gillian Bristow and Adrian Healy (2016), Measuring regional economic resilience across Europe: operationalizing a complex concept, *Spatial Economic Analysis*, Vol. 11, Number 2, pp. 128–151.

Silim, Amna (2016), *What is New Economic Thinking: Three strands of Heterodox Economics that are Leading the Way*, evonomics.com, 19 August (retrieved 3 January 2017).

Simmons, Beth A. and Zachary Elkins (2004), The globalization of liberalization: policy diffusion in the international political economy, *American Political Science Review*, Vol. 98, Number 1, pp. 171–189.

Sinclair, Scott (2011), The WTO and its GATS, in J. Michie (ed.), *The Handbook of*

Globalisation, 2nd edition, Cheltenham, UK and Northampton, MA, USA: Edward Elgar Publishing, Chapter 21.

Sinclair, Scott, Hadrian Mertins-Kirkwood and Stuart Trew (2016), *Making Sense of CETA*, 2nd edition, Ontario: Canadian Centre for Policy Alternatives.

Singh, Ajit and Ann Zammitt (2011), Globalisation, Labour Standards And Economic Development, in J. Michie (ed.), *The Handbook of Globalisation*, 2nd edition, Cheltenham, UK and Northampton, MA, USA: Edward Elgar Publishing, Chapter 12.

Smith, Adam (1776), *Wealth of Nations*, London: Methuen & Co (1904, 5th edition).

Sraffa, Piero (1926), The laws of return under competitive conditions, *Economic Journal*, Vol. 36, pp. 535-550.

Standing, Guy (2011), *The Precariat: The New Dangerous Class*, London & New York: Bloomsbury Academic.

Standing, Guy (2014), *A Precariat Charter: From Denizens to Citizens*, London & New York: Bloomsbury Academic.

Stanford, Jim (2011), The North American Free Trade Agreement: Context, Structure And Performance, in J. Michie (ed.), *The Handbook of Globalisation*, 2nd edition, Cheltenham, UK and Northampton, MA, USA: Edward Elgar Publishing, Chapter 16.

Stiglitz, Joseph (2002), *Globalization and its Discontents*, London: W.W. Norton.

Stiglitz, Joseph (2015), *Rewriting the Rules of the American Economy: An Agenda for Growth and Shared Prosperity*, London: W.W. Norton.

Stiglitz, Joseph (2016a), *The Euro And Its Threat to the Future of Europe*, London: Allen Lane.

Stiglitz, Joseph (2016b), *Globalization and its New Discontents*, project-syndicate.org, 5 August (retrieved 3 January 2017).

Storper, Michael (1992), The limits to globalization: technology districts and international trade, *Economic Geography*, Vol. 68, Number 1, pp. 60-93.

Storper, Michael, Thomas Kemeny, Naji P. Makarem and Taner Osman (2016), On specialization, divergence and evolution: a brief response to Ron Martin's review, *Regional Studies*, Vol. 50, Number 9, pp. 1628-1629.

Summers, L. (2016), Interest rates are at inconceivable levels, and we must confront what that means, WONKBLOG, *The Washington Post*, 6 July.

Sutcliffe, Bob and Andrew Glyn (2011), Measures of Globalisation and Their Misinterpretation, in J. Michie (ed.), *The Handbook of Globalisation*, 2nd edition, Cheltenham, UK and Northampton, MA, USA: Edward Elgar Publishing, Chapter 4.

Swank, Duane (1998), Funding the welfare state: globalization and the taxation of business in advanced market economies, *Political Studies*, Vol. 46, Number 4, pp. 671-692.

Swyngedouw, Erik (2004), Globalisation or 'glocalisation'? Networks, territories and rescaling, *Cambridge Review of International Affairs*, Vol. 17, Number 1, pp. 25-48.

Tarrow, Sidney (2001), Transnational politics: contention and institutions in international politics, *Annual Review of Political Science*, Vol. 4, Number 1, pp. 1-20.

Taylor, Mark Zachary (2016), *The Politics of Innovation: Why Some Countries are Better than Others at Science & Technology*, Oxford: Oxford University Press.

Teulings, C. and R. Baldwin (2014), *Secular Stagnation: Facts, Causes and Cures*, voxeU. org (retrieved 3 January 2017).

Thompson, Grahame (2011), Financial Globalization? History, Conditions and Prospects, in J. Michie (ed.), *The Handbook of Globalisation*, 2nd edition, Cheltenham, UK and Northampton, MA, USA: Edward Elgar Publishing, Chapter 2.

Tischer, Daniel, Ruth Yeoman, Stuart White, Alex Nicholls and Jonathan Michie (2016), An evaluative framework for mutual and employee-owned businesses, *Journal of Social Entrepreneurship*, Vol. 7, Number 3, pp. 342–68.

Tisdell, Clem (2001), Globalisation and sustainability: environmental Kuznets curve and the WTO, *Ecological Economics*, Vol. 39, Number 2, pp. 185–196.

Townsend, Mike (2016), *Coming of Age: The Heroes and Villains of the Circular Economy*, edie.net, 15 August (retrieved 3 January 2017).

Townsend, Mike (2017), *The Quiet Revolution*, London: Greenleaf.

Toye, John (2011), The International Monetary Fund and the World Bank, in J. Michie (ed.), *The Handbook of Globalisation*, 2nd edition, Cheltenham, UK and Northampton, MA, USA: Edward Elgar Publishing, Chapter 22.

Tyson, Laura and Anu Madgavkar (2016), *The Great Income Stagnation*, project-syndicate.org, 7 September (retrieved 3 January 2017).

Tyson, Laura and Lenny Mendonca (2016), *Fighting Poverty in America*, project-syndicate.org, 27 July (retrieved 3 January 2017).

ul Haq, Mahbub, Inge Kaul and Isabelle Grunberg (eds) (1996), *The Tobin Tax: Coping with Financial Volatility*, Oxford: Oxford University Press.

United Nations (2009), *Report of the Commission of Experts of the President of the United Nations General Assembly on Reforms of the International Monetary and Financial System*, New York: United Nations.

United Nations (2010), *United Nations Millennium Declaration*, General Assembly Resolution 55/2, New York: United Nations.

United Nations Environment Programme (2008), *Green New Deal*, New York: United Nations.

United Nations Framework Convention on Climate Change (2010), *Outcome of the Work of the Ad Hoc Working Group on Long-term Cooperative Action under the Convention*, Decision 1/Cp. 16, Cancun.

United States Government (2001), *Economic Report of the President 2001*, Washington, DC: United States Government.

Vernon, Raymond (1966), International investment and international trade in the product cycle, *The Quarterly Journal of Economics*, Vol. 80, Number 2, pp. 190–207.

Voegele, Juergen and John Roome (2016), The challenge to be smart with the world's agriculture, blogs.worldbank.org, 11 August (retrieved 3 January 2017).

Wade, Robert (2009), From global imbalances to global reorganization, *Cambridge Journal of Economics*, Vol. 33, Number 4, pp. 539–562.

Wade, Robert Hunter (2004), Is globalization reducing poverty and inequality?, *World Development*, Vol. 32, Number 4, pp. 567–589.

Waters, Sarah and Jenny Chan (2016), *How Work can lead to Suicide in a Globalized Economy*, theconverstion.com, 16 August (retrieved 3 January 2017).

Whitmarsh, Lorraine (2011), Social and Psychological Drivers of Energy Consumption Behavior and Energy Transitions, in S. Dietz, J. Michie and C. Oughton (eds), *The Political Economy of the Environment*, London: Routledge, Part III, Chapter 11.

Wilkinson, Richard and Kate Pickett (2009), *The Spirit Level: Why More Equal Societies Almost Always Do Better*, London: Penguin.

Williamson, J. (1993), Democracy and the 'Washington Consensus', *World Development*, Vol. 21, Number 8, pp. 1329–1336.

Wilson, David Sloan (2016), *'My Nation First!' is No Better than 'Me First!'*, evonomics. com, 30 July (retrieved 3 January 2017).

Wolf, Martin (2016), The tide of globalisation is turning, *Financial Times*, 30 August.

Wood, Adrian (1994), *North–South Trade, Employment and Inequality: Changing Fortunes in a Skill-Driven World*, Oxford: Clarendon Press.

Wood, Adrian (1998), Globalisation and the rise in labour market inequalities, *The Economic Journal*, Vol. 108, Number 450, pp. 1463–1482.

Woodward, Richard (2011), Governance in a Globalised World, in J. Michie (ed.), *The Handbook of Globalisation*, 2nd edition, Cheltenham, UK and Northampton, MA, USA: Edward Elgar Publishing, Chapter 18.

World Commission on Environment and Development (1987), *Our Common Future (The Brundtland Report)*, Oxford: Oxford University Press.

Young, Alasdair R. (2016), Not your parents' trade politics: the Transatlantic Trade and Investment Partnership negotiations, *Review of International Political Economy*, Vol. 23, Number 3, June, pp. 345–378.

Zamagni, Vera Negri and Stefano Zamagni (2010), *Cooperative Enterprise: Facing the Challenge of Globalization*, Cheltenham, UK and Northampton, MA, USA: Edward Elgar Publishing.

Index

Titles in the **Elgar Advanced Introductions** series include:

International Political Economy
Benjamin J. Cohen

The Austrian School of Economics
Randall G. Holcombe

Cultural Economics
Ruth Towse

Law and Development
Michael J. Trebilcock and Mariana Mota Prado

International Humanitarian Law
Robert Kolb

International Tax Law
Reuven S. Avi-Yonah

Post Keynesian Economics
J.E. King

International Intellectual Property
Susy Frankel and Daniel J. Gervais

Public Management and Administration
Christopher Pollitt

Organised Crime
Leslie Holmes

Nationalism
Liah Greenfeld

Social Policy
Daniel Béland and Rianne Mahon

Consumer Behaviour Analysis
Gordon Foxall

International Conflict and Security Law
Nigel D. White

Comparative Constitutional Law
Mark Tushnet

International Human Rights Law
Dinah L. Shelton

Entrepreneurship
Robert D. Hisrich

International Trade Law
Michael J. Trebilcock

Public Policy
B. Guy Peters

The Law of International Organizations
Jan Klabbers

International Environmental Law
Ellen Hey

International Sales Law
Clayton P. Gillette

Corporate Venturing
Robert D. Hisrich

Public Choice
Randall G. Holcombe

Private Law
Jan M. Smits

Globalisation
Jonathan Michie